CIRCUMSTANTIAL EVIDENCE

CIRCUMSTANTIAL EVIDENCE

By

JASON LIVELY

Published by BMF.publishing, LLC

BMF.publishing@yahoo.com

Cover by Lori P. Lay

Edited by Betty Tucker

Copyright 2014 by Charles Jason Lively

All rights reserved. This book is sold under the condition that it shall not by way of trade, be copied, lent, resold, hired out, or circulated without the author and publisher's written consent.

This is a work of fiction, names, characters, places, and incidents are products of the author's imagination and are not real. He draws inspiration from family, friends, life experiences, and stories told and heard over many years. Some of the places may seem familiar, characters as well, but they are not real. Any resemblance to actual persons living or dead, events, or locales are not intentional.

ISBN-978-0-9960328-2-7 (BMF.publishing, LLC)

I want to thank, Billie, the owner of BMF.publishing for believing in me, without her, none of this would be possible. Also, my Mother and family for all of their support, and a special thanks to my Aunt Betty.

"If you're going through hell, keep going."

Winston Churchill

CORRESPONDENCE FROM AN INMATE AT MOUNTAIN TOP CORRECTIONAL COMPLEX

Jessie,

    How have you been? I know it's been a while since I have written. I've had a lot on my mind and haven't been writing like I should. It's been harder than usual these last couple of months waiting to hear something that may end up being my salvation. Billie's presence has made it easier to cope. Together with Mom they have started a Facebook page for me and a petition asking the governor for a pardon. After Casey was acquitted, the prosecutor hired an expert fire investigator to review my case. In his report he says it wasn't arson. Without arson there is no murder. I can't believe I haven't been released yet. I guess it is foolish of me to think someone would actually do the right thing.

    I have been thinking about our childhood, all of the things we use to do and how innocent it all was. Did you ever imagine I would end up like this? It's a long way from where I started. It all came so easy growing up, and through school, now I'm in a constant struggle. Everything was good until Dad died. He would be real proud of how I turned out, huh? A convicted murderer! I ask myself every day, how I could have let myself get into the shape I'm in. I got into a few fist fights and other kinds of meanness, but I have always respected my elders, women, and looked out for little kids. What I can't understand is even though the prosecutor has proof of my innocence, I'm still being held prisoner. What really eats at me is I can't do anything about it.

 I don't know if you have read, "The Tale of Two Cities," by Charles Dickens, but if you haven't -you need to. It's about an innocent man that was imprisoned, lost his mind, only to be rescued by his daughter years later. Everything was new and scary to him, but his daughter stuck by him and with her love - brought him back to his senses. It ends by him sacrificing himself for her well - being. There is one part in the book when the old man describes looking at the moon through a small window in his cell, what he thought and was reminded of when he looked at "her." He says, "I have looked at her from my prison window when I could not bear her light. I have looked at her when it has been such torture to me to think of her shining upon what I have lost, that I have beat my head against my prison wall." I have thought and felt that way hundreds of times since I have been in prison (kidnapped). For the most part I try not to look out of my window, especially during the day. Mostly because it's depressing to acknowledge the world is still turning without being in it. I do, however, like to look at the moon whenever it shows itself out my little window. It draws me to it like a moth to a flame. It's like a kindred spirit that shares in my loneliness. Like that old cliché about the moon and the question of, is the one I love looking at the same moon at the same time I am? In my deprived state that makes sense, crazy right? This is how I relate; the moon is the connecting point between me, faith, love, and hope. It's like the moon connects me and my dreams to bring them all together for one brief moment. It gives me that hope and closeness I so desperately need. I'm glad none of my fellow prisoners can read what I just wrote to you. If they did I'm sure I would have a couple of them trying to beat me up and a couple trying to make friends (if you know what I mean). Needless to say, it would spur some unwanted attention! Well, Jess, I'm going to get back to it. I have been writing to occupy my mind and time. I'll let you know how it turns out. Tell everyone I said hello and I love and miss them.

Your Loyal Brother,

Charlie

Chapter 1

Growing up in the 80's in southern West Virginia was like no other place on earth. Most of our neighbors had lived in the mountains for generations: coming down the mountain to work, cash their meager paychecks, shop, and pay bills. They were honest hard-working folks-coal miners or retired miners. Occasionally some of them found work as a logger. We all coexisted on the "The Mountain." We called it, "The Mountain," for the obvious reason that it was located in the Appalachian mountain range between the West Virginia-Virginia border.

Our closest neighbors, my mother's brother and his family, lived about a half of a mile away. Uncle Jr. was a boss in the coal mines, a no-nonsense hard working family man. His wife, my Aunt Alice, was a stay-at-home mom who was always busy doing something: cleaning, washing dishes, taking care of my cousins, Jessie and Angie. I never once heard them say a cross word to one another or even raise their voices. It always seemed like they knew exactly what the other one was going to say. They were in perfect harmony with one another.

Being an only child and not having other kids nearby, Jessie and I became very close. In fact, we were more like brothers than cousins. His sister, Angie, and I fought like brothers and sisters, maybe more so than she and Jessie.

Uncle Jr., like my grandpa Halsey, fought chickens in his free time. In fact, he owned and operated a chicken fighting pit. Even though I don't think he ever made any money, he continued to do it, because that's what he loved to do.

I remember spending the night with Jessie the day before the fights so I could go with him. We liked being one of the first ones there. We would get up well before day break, because we had to take the supplies for the concession stand and get things ready for the upcoming fights. Jessie and I would help as much as we could and tried our best not to get in the way. The fights, which were only held every other weekend, were as much of a social gathering as it was a sporting event. When you live in a place as secluded as, "the mountain," you look for any reason to get together, because the chances to socialize are few and far between. The fights would start early in the morning and last the better part of the day; depending on how many people decided to enter into that weekend's fight. Jessie and I would busy ourselves looking at the chickens and betting among ourselves. The times when we couldn't get a bet, the older men would usually take our bet just so we could join in on the fun. The good thing about that was if we lost they usually wouldn't take our money. If they did, they would see us later in the day and give it back to us, generally with a little advice or betting tip to go with it.

The big thing among the kids was pitching quarters, which was kind of like a rite of passage. If you were good at pitching quarters you were the cock of the walk and, therefore, graduated to betting on the cock fights with all of the rest of the grownups.

On the mountain there was no cable and in the summer water was scarce. So if you had water during June and July you didn't waste it, but shared freely with the neighbors. We only had two channels on the TV. Sometimes we could get an extra station if the weather was nice and if you were lucky enough to have a good strong antenna. For only one more channel, most households didn't buy the more expensive antennas. There were more important pursuits than TV.

Mom and Dad were friends with a couple, Dennis and Donna, who lived around the ridge a few miles away. Donna worked with my mother at the clinic and they had two children. Even though I can remember Dennis and Donna coming over, I barely remember the kids. Because there was no cable TV, Dennis would always bring his guitar, and play while Donna sang. It made me feel like we were the luckiest and most well-off family on "The Mountain". I loved to watch him play: he made it look so easy. I could see the music flowing through his fingers as he would pluck out song after song. He seemed like the happiest man in the world when he had that guitar in his hands. I heard mom and dad talk about how Ralph Stanley had offered him a job, but he wouldn't take it because he wouldn't leave Donna and the kids. Dennis liked to drink which contributed to them divorcing. He often said nothing or no-one could tear him away from her. Even after their marriage was over, he still held onto the hope of getting back together.

Growing up, we always had a bulldog: the fighting kind, not the fat, stubbed nosed ones that are the mascots of so many college sports teams. People's perception of pit bulls as mean, blood thirsty, fighting dogs, is not realistic. Some were trained, like soldiers, to fight. My dad did fight, train, and breed dogs, but I loved them because of their strength and loyalty.

I grew up with this one particular dog, Buck, who was born about the same time as me. Our entire family loved him very much. Dad trained Buck to fight and would bet his entire paycheck on him. Dad said Buck was a winner, because he had the most heart. Buck never lost and was a source of income for our family. One we counted on that was as sure as the sun coming up tomorrow. Above all else, Buck was a family pet and I use to ride him like a horse and wrestle with him. To get him to do something you only had to speak to him in a normal voice, and you never had to repeat yourself. It was amazing how well he listened and behaved, considering his training and capabilities.

One time after a fight where he had gotten chewed up pretty badly, Dad kept him in the house for a couple of weeks to recuperate. I remember crying, begging Dad not to make Buck fight; I was so scared he was going to get killed. When Dad came home and told me Buck won and was going to be allowed to stay in the house while he healed, I was tickled to death. The only thing was I couldn't play with him because he was hurt. I made him a little bed in the corner of the living room behind the coal burning stove where he would be out of the way, but could still see everything that went on. For two days he never moved except to eat and drink a little water. On the third day he was starting to move around a little more, Mom and Dad finally allow me to pet him. Mom said that he would be back to his old self in a couple more days: that he was healing well, but would be sore for a while. I was reminded at least a dozen times to be careful about how I was petting him. Every time I would accidently hit one of his sore spots he would whimper or look up at me with this pitiful look. The next morning I was up before everyone else and took Buck food and water. When I sat it down his tail started wagging, his ears perked up and he made short work of the food. I forgot all about his wounds when he started licking me and I wanted to wrestle. I started slapping at him, grabbing his jowls and shook him to get him riled up, but he didn't want to play and even barked at me - which was very unusual. I never remember him barking at me before. I grabbed his jowls again and started shaking him, only this time he pinned me to the ground. He had his front paws on my shoulders and was growling, but it wasn't like his face was in my face. He reminded me of a wolf when they throw their head back and howl. It scared me to the bottom of my soul. I remember Dad running into the room, and as soon as Buck saw him, he got off me and went over to his bed and hunkered down. The barking woke him up and as soon as he heard Buck growling he knew what was happening. Buck didn't want to hurt me, but he didn't want me to hurt him either. The bark was a cry for help. He only pinned me down because I wouldn't stop and that was his only way to get help. He knew Mom and Dad would come running if they heard me crying which to Buck was the same as a bark. Lassie could learn a lot from old Buck!

We always had at least four or five adult dogs which produced a few litters of pups every year. Like any kid, I loved the bulldog pups because they were especially rowdy and high strung. So, I was used to getting bit and scratched. When the pups were big enough to be taken from their mothers, Mom would let me keep one in the house every now and then. Dad bought a pup from one of his dog fighting buddies. It was solid black with four white feet and a diamond on his chest. This particular puppy was extremely expensive and Dad still owed the man a couple hundred dollars for it. Since he was too small to put on a chain, I got to keep him in the house. I even had my own leash for him when I took him outside for a walk or to use the bathroom. We couldn't let him run loose for fear of him getting too close to one of the other dogs and getting killed. One day as I was taking him for his walk, Mom reminded me, "don't let Buck get close to that puppy or he will kill him, and your daddy will throw a fit." I went to see Buck, because I hadn't been down to play with him in a few days. I thought I could tie the leash to a tree or, if all else failed; hold the pup in one hand while I petted Buck with the other. When Buck saw me coming he got excited and started wagging his tail a hundred miles an hour. I ran up to him wanting to play, but I couldn't find anything safe to tie the little pup to. The pup was scared of Buck, so he kept his distance on the leash. As a precaution I held the leash as far away from Buck as I could, while I was petting him. I suppose the puppy got his courage up and grew comfortable enough to get close. One thing I didn't take into consideration was the leash was at least six feet long, and I had a wing span of about four feet. So, there was two feet of the leash more than I could account for, and as soon as he got close enough Buck snatched him. I can still hear the sound of its little bones breaking as Buck and I played tug of war with the little yelping dog. I had hold of the leash pulling with all my might one way and Buck had a hold of the pup pulling the other. Suddenly the collar broke and Buck shook and chewed the pup like he was an old shoe. I still remember that feeling of helplessness and dread the instant that collar broke. All I could do was watch Buck shake that little puppy like a dish rag. I ran back to the house as fast as I could; Dad was just getting out of bed and I told him what happened. He ran to where we kept Buck, but I knew it was too late. He came back carrying the dead dog, cussing like a sailor, telling me he had told me a hundred times not to let that pup get around any of the other dogs.

We had an old barn that Dad used as a fighting and training ring. To strengthen their jaws and necks, Dad had attached a big spring to the ceiling with a groundhog hide (super durable and less hair than a raccoon or deer) tied to it, just out of reach of the dogs when they were standing on their hind legs. They would jump up, grab the hide and while they were either hanging in mid-air or barely touching the ground, they would start to shake and pull on it. The hides were easier on their teeth than other materials. Groundhog hides were not all that easy to find. I recall several times driving down the road and Dad would see a groundhog either setting on the side of the road or crossing it. The next thing I knew we would be in the other lane or in the ditch line trying to run over it. I can't tell you how many fenders he hair-lipped or tires he busted trying to run over those groundhogs, but it was a few. Mom use to talk and joke about how expensive those groundhogs were and suggested he buy a gun because bullets were a lot cheaper than tires.

In the back of this old barn Dad had a small marijuana garden, although I didn't understand what it was at the time. I didn't recognize it was something illegal or bad. He would roll joints and smoke pot like they were cigarettes. I never made a distinction between the two. I did think it was odd that the "cigarette" was shared among others and no one had their own.

If I was up before Mom left for work on the week-ends, she would wake Dad to let him know she was leaving, and that I was up. When I could get Dad out of bed, he would watch cartoons with me-even if it was only a show or two. Sometimes I would give up on him, especially if Mom wasn't working. Then I would talk her into watching a few shows with me or until Dad got up.

On one of those weekends that Mom had to work, I pestered Dad until he gave up trying to sleep and got up to watch cartoons with me. Dennis and Donna had been over the night before and stayed later than usual, so I'm sure he was a little hung over and hadn't had much sleep. During the first commercial he asked me to go to the refrigerator and get him a bottle of soda. We bought Cokes in tall 16 ounce glass bottles back then and, by mistake, I brought him back what was left of the wine from the night before. He said, "Son, this isn't soda, but I'll drink it." He called it "hair of the dog"! It wasn't long before he was rolling himself a joint. I don't know if you are familiar with the side effects of marijuana, but it affects your short term memory. Actions are more out of habit and reflex than anything cognitive. So, here I am, five-maybe even six years old, watching cartoons with my dad, who has only been up for thirty minutes at the very most, he only had a few hours' sleep and was about half hung over. On top of all that, he had drunk half a bottle of wine and smoked about half a joint when, by mistake, he passed the joint to me. I didn't say a word, but took it from him like an old pro who had done it countless times before. I hit it like I've seen him and others do so many times before and since. I don't know if I coughed or if he started looking for the joint, that he noticed it was gone. I may have even tried to pass it back to him and it dawned on him what he had done. I froze when I saw the surprised look on his face. It can only be described as a look of uncertainty and embarrassment.

I had never seen him look as vulnerable as the reality of his screw up sunk in. He couldn't get mad at me, but he did let me know what I had done was wrong and to never do it again. We talked about it when I was older. He told me that he didn't think I would have even felt any of the effects since I could have only taken a puff or two before he noticed what he had done. Besides, I probably didn't even inhale, so what was the worst that could happen. Apparently I did inhale, because he said he had never seen me laugh so hard. I remember my sides and stomach being sore for days afterward. That was mine and my father's first real secret. Up till now, I never told anyone, because of the look on his face when he realized what he had done. I was like every other kid in my thinking that my father was invincible, and could do no wrong. I never wanted to believe anything to the contrary. Dad had a simple way of talking to me and explaining things so I could understand what he was trying to say. He didn't sugar coat anything nor did he treat me like a child: maybe that was the key to my understanding him so well.

My mother on the other hand was more of an authority figure. She worked hard and made sure I had everything I needed and most of what I wanted. It's hard to give a good example of the differences between them at that age, but I knew I could get by with a lot more with Dad than I could Mom. Mom would have busted my ass if she would have seen me puffing on that joint. Hell, she and Dad would have been in a no-holds barred fist fight. I remember coming home from Jessie's one day and walking in on the middle of one of their UFC bouts. I saw Dad hit her so hard it knocked her to the ground, but she bounced up so fast you would have thought she had a spring tied to her ass and flew right back in at him swinging with both fists. Needless to say, that was a major factor in keeping mine and Dad's secret.

My cousin Jessie and I both had ponies. Our parents would cut us loose and allow us to ride around the ridge and on the road going along "The Mountain." We didn't really have set boundaries. The only rule was we had to stay together. We knew where we could go and where we couldn't. Common sense was our boundary and guide. Whenever we would get hungry or thirsty, we only had to stop at the next house. That was the good thing about living on "The Mountain." Everyone knew everyone else and treated their neighbor like they wanted to be treated and their neighbor's children like they would their own. If we stopped somewhere to get a drink of water or just to say hello it was hard if not all together impossible to get away without eating something. I don't know whatever happened to my pony, whether he was sold, traded off, or if he died. I know my parents use to say that I was riding him to death, so he may have died, like I said, I don't remember. I do remember that my cousin, Jessie's, pony died. I was so envious of his solid white pony. I thought it was the most beautiful pony in the whole world. Everyone gave him compliments on how pretty he was, but Jessie never bragged. Every now and then, he would trade out with me, and let me ride his pony for a while.

Somewhere along the line I ended up with a motorcycle. It was an RM-80 and much too big for me. I guess Dad figured I would grow into it. I couldn't even touch the pegs: my feet just dangled from the seat. I rode it like a horse with no saddle, gripping the seat with my thighs! Changing gears or using the back break was completely out of the question. Dad would put it in second gear, set me on it, and push me off to a rolling start like a child when first learning to ride a bicycle. It wasn't long before I got the hang of riding, but not being able to go any faster than 10 or 15 mph wasn't cutting it anymore. One day I heard him explaining to Mom that he put the motorcycle in a lower gear so I wouldn't get hurt if I wrecked. Mom gave Dad a hard time over letting me ride a motorcycle that was obviously too big for me, but at this point in their marriage, I think he mostly allowed me to ride it just to piss her off. I can remember the arguments getting more frequent, and they would often lead to out and out fist fights. She started seeing how well I could ride and noticed the only time I ever "wrecked" was when I tried to turn a corner too slow and then the bike only fell over. I would see her watching me from the porch with that concerned and worried look that constantly reminded me to be careful. I believe she would have put a stop to me riding, if she didn't know how much I loved it and how happy it made me. She would, however, make Dad stop me and check what gear I had the motorcycle. She said, "It looks like he keeps getting faster and faster on that thing." Eventually he would give in and check just to pacify her, but it was almost impossible to tell because the shifter would stick and even get caught between gears. He also suspected I had found a way to change the gears on my own. It wasn't long before he caught me. I had a path around the house. When I got to the backside where no one could see me, or so I thought, I would lean all the way over until my foot reached the peg and I could get enough balance and stability to change the gears. I had to lean over so far that the only thing that kept me from falling off before I reached the peg was my other foot that was hooked behind the opposite side of the gas tank. I must have been a sight, because when Dad saw me he only laughed and told me to be careful. He warned me that if Mom saw me she would take my motorcycle away. Whenever I started to run out of gas or when it was getting too dark to ride anymore, I would pull up next to the porch and stop so I could get off and lean my motorcycle on the side of the porch. It was like my personal step ladder. I only needed Dad to start it for me. Weighing 50 pounds at the most, I couldn't kick start it myself.

    I only have one other memory of the time before my parents divorced and my mother and I moved off "The Mountain." Dad was working on the car and I was standing at the back door when I heard a strange thud. I saw Dad come walking toward the back door holding his chest with both hands. I could tell immediately there was something wrong, even without seeing the blood that had stained the front of his shirt and saturated his jeans. I ran for Mom and by the time I found her and returned to the back door Dad was coming up the steps. Ghostly pale and in obvious pain, Mom helped him to the bathroom, and tore his shirt off so she could examine and clean the wound. I can still see her as she took control in that calm, cool manner, and it made me think, feel, and know everything was going to be alright. Before she ran me out of the bathroom, I did see the hole in my father's chest. It was reflected in the bathroom mirror as my mother poured what could have only been alcohol or peroxide over the wound in his blood soaked chest. A piece of metal that came off the alternator was struck in my father's chest. The doctor said it only missed his heart by an eighth of an inch and if it wasn't for mom keeping him immobile, he could have very easily punctured his heart and died. It was only then that I realized that my mother was a nurse and imagined her at work saving lives and helping people just like she did Dad. You couldn't tell me anything after that. I knew nothing could hurt me. If I did get hurt, I only had to wait until Mom got home from work, and she would fix it.

Chapter 2

It wasn't long after that my parents were divorced. Since my mom got full custody of me and the place on "The Mountain", my dad had little choice but to stay at my grandmother's. I went to school and stayed with her during the week, then went to Dads on the weekend. It was a good arrangement, especially for me, because it was always something new and exciting. I thought of it as an adventure and it made me feel special. A big plus was not having to watch and listen to them fight and argue all the time. This arrangement also gave Mom some much needed rest when she didn't have to work. When Dad had to go somewhere he couldn't take me or went out to the club, I got to stay with my grandma Pangloss. I always had something to do or somewhere to go: it was never boring. It wasn't long before we moved off "The Mountain" and into town. It was getting cold out and hard to gather enough wood and coal to last through the winter. It was damn near impossible to keep the water from freezing. With Mom working, me starting first grade, and no one at home, our little heating stove would often go completely out before we made it home. Anyone who has any experience with those old coal stoves knows it's much easier to rekindle a fire than to start one from scratch.

It was hard to say when Mom would get off of work because the doctor would have her work late or stay around to discuss politics. Her boss was very political and he used Mom like she was his political assistant: especially if it was an election year. She received no additional pay for all her extra work! A single mother does not want to come home after working all day to a cold house and have to start a fire after packing enough wood and coal in to last the rest of the night. I was too small to be of much help when it came to packing wood or five gallon buckets of coal. I remember several mornings getting up to a cold house because Mom was so exhausted that she fell asleep without remembering to stoke the fire. When we would get home she would build a fire, get me bathed and ready for bed. Then get in enough coal and wood for the rest of the night. If she set down to rest for one second she would fall asleep and most of the time wouldn't wake up until the next morning. Then it was time to do it all over again, and no use in building a fire because it would be time to leave before the house had time to get warm. The winters were so cold on top of that mountain the water would freeze if you didn't leave the water running a little. The trick was to only run as big of a stream as necessary without wasting it, because even though the water wasn't as apt to run out in the winter, it did happen. So we still had to conserve as much as we could without letting the stream get so small it would freeze.

We moved to town and into a one bedroom apartment that was located over the Ben Franklin's Five and Dime store. We had only one neighbor, an older lady who minded her own business. I only remember seeing her a few times in the three years we lived there and one of those times was the first day while we were carrying our things inside. She told us that, "you'll soon get use to these trains, and won't be able to sleep without them." Well, it wasn't soon enough! It was hell; the trains ran constantly day and night. Our apartment was located between two railroad crossings, one on each end of town and the town is only three or four hundred yards long. So they would start blowing their horns way before they got to either railroad crossing. They would continue all the way through town and kept on blowing even after they passed the last crossing: either out of spite, or habit, which I'm not sure. Our neighbor turned out to be right, because I grew so accustomed to them it was hard for me to fall asleep when I spent the weekends with Dad.

In the mid to late 80's our little town still had several stores and a few restaurants. Since we lived close to Mom's work and my school, I didn't have to get up at 5:00 a.m. to get to school by 8:00 a.m. Mom also got to sleep later, plus she didn't have to deal with those roads or that coal stove any longer. I knew it was more convenient and am sure she liked it better, especially now that she was a single parent.

It was a lot different than what I was accustomed to; I liked the change. We now had cable television and my cousin Jessie, and I would set up watching movies all night; whenever we could talk Uncle Jr. into letting him spend the night with me. There was a pizza place and movie rental just up the street from us. Mom arranged credit at both places for me. I loved movies and pizza so I was in heaven. The movie place would even call me first whenever they got in new releases or a movie I wanted came in. I only lived a few hundred feet down the street and would be there in a flash. For me things couldn't be any better or different.

I've heard people say how hard divorce is for children, but I think it was harder on my parents than it was on me. I know it was harder on my father, one minute he would be calling Mom a bitch and a whore, but in the same breath he would say how much he loved and missed her.

After a couple years when I was a little older, and more comfortable with town life, I convinced Mom to let me stay by myself until she came home from work. Until then I stayed with my maternal grandparents. There was only an hour overlap between me coming home from school and Mom's arrival from work. On some afternoons, Mom would have to work over and I could stretch my hour into three. This was my alone time. Since we lived in a one bedroom apartment and I didn't have my own bedroom, this was a time I really enjoyed having to myself. I had the added bonus of having a house key. I liked the responsibility and it made me feel like a grown up. To keep from losing it I ran it through my bottom shoe lace where I knew it would be safe.

On the weekend I would go to Dads which meant I also got to see Mamaw (that's what everyone called her-especially her grandchildren). On most Friday and Saturday nights Dad would go to the local bar. He would be out of the house and on his way by 10:00 pm at the latest. Mamaw said he was going out "cat birding." I still don't know where she got that from?

She would spoil me more than most of her other grandchildren, but that may have been because I was always around. Well, me and my cousin, Chris. He and his mom lived next door to Mamaw. His parents had the same arrangement as mine. He stayed at his father's during the weekend and with his mother during the week. He was a little younger than me, but we got along well enough. We were constantly competing for Mamaw's attention. I remember us fighting over who would be the one to rub lotion on her feet. Her legs and feet would swell from standing all day. The longer she was on her feet the more they would swell. I think it had to do with her heart condition. Since it was difficult for her to bend over, anytime we could we would do it for her we did. When Chris and I would start fighting over who was going to rub lotion on her feet she would tell us, "If you two don't behave I'm going to split you up." A whipping was never a serious threat so she came up with that splitting us up thing, which I can only remember her doing once. We all knew there wasn't anything she wouldn't do for any of us so we looked for any and every opportunity to take care of her. She had this quality about her, you could see the loving kindness radiating through her. She really was a saint if there ever was one! Dad use to say, "She's the best woman I know." The advice she gave was always spot on. She told the best stories whether it was one out of the Bible or about her growing up during the great depression. She was truly a remarkable woman with knowledge that could only come through experience. She is one of the few people who I can say was truly wise.

Mamaw and I would set up and watch Johnny Carson and The Golden Girls. I loved to watch her laugh. We would also watch wrestling, but we stopped because she said they cheated. Hulk Hogan was her favorite wrestler because he would whip the bad guys and stood for what was right. I can still hear her say, "You just wait until the Hulk comes out." If you came in the house between 1:00 p.m. and 4:00 p.m. you would find her in "her chair" watching "her stories." If you made the mistake of turning the channel you would have hell to pay. Afterwards she would tell whoever it was that was foolish enough to do such a thing, "you can think about turning it, just don't do it."

There were many times when Dad would come home after being out at the club all night and wake me up to talk. It would be 4:00 am and there we were talking and telling stories. That's the thing I miss the most. Those talks were beautiful: a father and son talking about everything and nothing while the rest of the world was sleeping. Whenever the weather permitted and the river was clear, we went fishing. We would talk for hours without even noticing we hadn't caught anything. I know I was my Dad's best friend because he acted and talked to me like I was. Maybe that's only what being a father is all about and maybe not, but that was what mine was to me. He was and still is my hero.

This was when my father and I started the ritual of our Sunday morning drives. They began as a necessity, but they were also functional, as well as, educational. Dad was staying at Mamaw's at the time and this was a way for us to be alone and in our own little world. We would ride around sometimes all day long talking and telling stories to one another, along with making plans for what we were going to do "next weekend." In between our talking and plan making we would stop off at one of his friend's house or at the local diner for lunch, and to see who we could see. This was his work, that's how he made money. For lack of a better word, he was hustling. Not necessarily drugs, but guns, cars, and just about anything else you can think of. The only criteria was it had to make money.

My father was notorious for picking up hitchhikers. He knew just about everyone he picked up though. We lived in a small community where everyone knows everyone else. I could always tell if they were a friend of my father's or if he respected them, because if he did he would tell me to "crawl in back." If he was just giving someone a ride and didn't particularly consider them a friend, he would tell me to "just sit tight" and "he can get in the back." To a young boy that was not yet a teen, sitting in the front seat while a grownup was in the back was a big deal. He did things like that all the time and it made me feel like the most important person in the world to him. No matter where we were or who the company was, I never felt excluded. After he would make a deal he would often explain to me the reason why he did this or that, especially if it had a hidden strategy behind it.

We would stop for gas or a soda that Dad and I would split. I can see the smile on his face as I handed the soda back to him like it was yesterday. It's what could have only been the smile of a proud father. He would often ask while still smiling, "you didn't spit in it did you?" I would usually stay in the car while he went in. There were usually some older boys hanging around outside the store. Dad had a reputation for being a tough guy, and because he was a regular at the bars around the area, he fought a lot and when he did he won in dramatic fashion. This gave him a certain reputation that these older boys looked up to and they would come over and try to make friends with me. When Dad returned they would try to talk and carry on a conversation with him. He tried to be friendly, but kept it short. He would then dismiss them by saying he was in a hurry and we would be off.

Once we were back on the road he would say, "I don't want you getting too friendly with that boy he's a "Punk." Just the tone of his voice and his demeanor when he said it was enough to make me understand that a "punk" was something I didn't want to be. From then on whenever I heard my father refer to someone as a punk, I knew I wasn't to associate myself with that person.

It took my father a while before he got his own place, but eventually he did. My parents still kept the same arrangement and I went to Dads every weekend. His new place wasn't the nicest in the world, but it was clean, and served the purpose. The only bad thing was he didn't have cable and the only movie he owned was "Purple Rain". Let's be honest, Prince can't act for shit! I don't know how many times I watched that damn tape, but I remember thinking that it had to break sooner or later. I knew every word to every scene and it wasn't by choice.

When Mom would drop me off she wouldn't get out of the car much less step inside. She and Dad would exchange waves if he saw or heard us pull up, and if he wasn't at the door or outside before Mom would leave I had to go make sure it was ok. One time in particular she had to drop me off a few hours earlier than usual, which she rarely did. Dad didn't have a phone so she couldn't call ahead to let him know I was coming early. Dad came to the door and waved her off as I came in.

There were three people in the kitchen that I had never seen before. Dad told me to "go watch TV", so I went to watch Prince try to act again. He also said, "Do not go into the kitchen for any reason, if you want something I'll get it." There was never anyone at Dad's when I was there and if they were he ran them off. The kitchen table was set off by itself in what only could be described as a dining room. For whatever reason, I went into the kitchen after being told not to. I guess curiosity got the better of me. Dad was at the stove cooking and two of the three men at the table were busy messing with a heap of white powder, while the other one was off by himself smoking a strange looking pipe. When I say strange looking, I mean it didn't look like the one I saw Sherlock Holmes smoking. Dad didn't know I was there until I opened the refrigerator door. On my way to the refrigerator I was trying to see what Dad was cooking because I was a little hungry and a lot curious. I couldn't figure out what he was making though. He had a mason jar setting in a pot of water on the stove, holding it by its top gently swirling it around. He would constantly lift it out of the water and examine the liquid inside. Then dip it back into the pot of water, all the while never ceasing to swirl the liquid inside.

When I opened the refrigerator door and Dad saw me standing there gazing at the contents inside, he cussed me all to hell and reminded me of what he said about not going into the kitchen. He told me to go into the living room, which I immediately did! A few minutes later he came into the living room, and scolded me for not doing what he said but he was much calmer than he was before. This broke my heart; I never did anything for him to get upset over. It was a rare occasion that he had to correct me at all. I never asked what he was cooking, who those men were, or what they were doing. I do remember going out to eat shortly after that and when we came back everyone was gone and things went back to normal.

Chapter 3

During my early teen years I picked up the habit of dipping snuff from one of my older cousins. Around this same time I also received braces and those two go together like oil and water. My mother was dead set against me dipping snuff. Not only because it caused mouth cancer, but because as she said, "I've spent too much money on your teeth for you to ruin them by putting that shit in your lip." I'll give her credit; she tried her damndest to keep me from it. My father didn't help her cause at all; he would buy me a can or two every weekend when I would go to his house or sneak me some if he was to come to one of my ball games. He would tell me, "Don't let your Mom catch you with that, you know there will be hell to pay if she does." At first she tried to explain that it was bad for me and would, maybe, give me a light spanking. After she saw that wasn't working the whippings got worse and worse. I think the lying and hiding was as much a factor as the actual dipping.

She would whip me like she was trying to exercise a demon out of my ass, but what she didn't know was that her belts were too light and thin to hurt. It wasn't until my aunt came over and she and Mom were goofing around that Mom swatted her with one of her "whipping belts" that she noticed she didn't react. She swatted her again, but this time even harder and she shoved it away like she would a fly. Mom asked, "Didn't that hurt?" My aunt replied, "why no," and took the belt from my mother and slapped her across the ass with it. It was like a light came on and I knew right then I was found out. Whenever she would whip me I would play it up for all it was worth and I couldn't help but think how "smart" I was. After that she started improvising, turning every day house hold items into literally the pains in my ass. She used anything up to, but not limited to, the dust pan and broom. It all came down to what was within reaching distance. I've been whipped with everything from a bottle of Windex to the cord of a toaster-with the toaster still attached. That toaster cord had the potential to hurt, but she couldn't get both arms moving at the same time. She would hold the toaster in one hand and the cord in the other. She could never find her rhythm.

There was a tree that grew so close to our apartment that its branches touched our building and easily reached our second story apartment window. In the spring and summer, we couldn't see out that one window because the limbs and leaves obstructed the view. Mom solved that problem little by little. Every time she caught me misbehaving or dipping snuff she would simply reach out the window, break off a switch. I took notice of her having to reach farther and farther out of the window each time a new switch was required. So, on top of breaking, hiding, and throwing the switches away, I would break off as big a piece of a limb as I could without being too obvious. It took some time, but between the two of us, she was unable to reach any more switches. It wasn't long after our neighbor cut the tree down. I guess he was waiting for Mom to top it for him first.

I thought I was on easy street after that, but it only inspired her creativity. It seemed like every where she went, I would see her testing out something new. It was like watching a batter picking out which baseball bat he was going to use. She would first test it's durability and then its balance by taking a few practice swings before deciding whether she was going to buy it or not. At one point she was using trim that was intended to go around the windows and doors. She had broken so many pieces that the carpenter didn't have enough to finish the job. So she had to rush to the hardware store to purchase more. I stopped misbehaving as much and got better at hiding the dipping, but no matter what she tried, I wouldn't "quit that snuff" as she used to say.

During the week days I was constantly involved in some sport or another; it only depended on which one was in season. My mother was very supportive and active in all my extracurricular activities. She was involved in every fund raiser and community event she could volunteer for. At one point, she was the district president of the little league where I played. She continued to be involved even though I started playing baseball at another level. There were not enough hours in the day for her to do all of the things she was committed to, but somehow she made it work.

In the summer she would let me stay with my dad and mamaw a little during the week and a little with my cousins. Dad said, "It's because she's out whoring around," which was not the case at all. She was working, but there was no use trying to explain this to my father. His mind was made up. That was his go to line, "she's out whoring around!"

My little cousin, Kenneth, and my maternal grandma and papaw lived side by side. (Kenneth had two brothers: Shea who was several years older than me and Keith, who was only a baby.) I call Kenneth "little Kenneth" not because he was so much younger than me, but because he wasn't very big for his age. His older brother, Shea, would give us a hard time every now and then but would always take up for us. I looked up to him, and he's the one who introduced me to dipping snuff. One time in junior high this guy was picking on me. He had been held back a few years and was closer to Shea's age and size than he was to mine. Every now and then, Shea would stop by at lunch on his way to vocational school to say hello. Just so happens this guy was picking on me, Shea got out of his car, and this guy said something slick, and Shea hit him in the mouth for it. The "tough guy" took off running to tell the principal. Shea got in all sorts of trouble for it. They band him from all basketball and football games and wouldn't let him participate in his graduation. He never said anything to me about all the trouble it caused him and I never forgot it. In my family cousins are about as close as brothers and sisters.

Kenneth and I played the same sports and were on the same teams. After school I would go to his house while mom was still at work. Well, actually I would go to my grandma and papaw's but like I said earlier, they lived side by side. Grandma would feed us and his mom or dad would take us to practice. My mom would pick us up and take him home.

I was good at whatever sport I chose to play, but after I felt like I was the best on the team, I stopped putting forth the same effort. Once I got to that point it made playing more enjoyable. I played because it came natural and was fun.

Mom and I moved a few times before I started high school. I was getting more rebellious and independent. I had even begun to smoke a little pot from time to time. Especially during the weekend at my dad's, (he had just bought a house beside my mamaw). I didn't have to hide smoking at his house. He told me he would rather me do it there so he knew where I was and who I was with. Mom and

I argued more and more, but very little of our arguments stemmed from my marijuana use. I think she was going through some things I didn't know about. Either way it was a volatile situation to say the least. Mom continued to work late and Doc, (what we called the doctor she worked for) wouldn't hesitate to call her at all hours of the night to do some kind of bullshit that "can't wait until tomorrow." It was mostly because he was lonely, and sometimes it was political nonsense. It may have been the lack of sleep that kept her so disagreeable, never the less our arguing continued.

Chapter 4

The conflict between my mother and me continued to worsen until I simply couldn't take it anymore. So one night, I snuck off to my father's house to live. To say I ran away from home would be incorrect. How could I run away from home to go home? They were both "my homes," so how could I run away? If I could have asked Mom to let me stay at Dads and she would have let me: I would have much rather went that route, but I know her and she wouldn't have allowed it.

I don't remember what day it was when I decided to walk to my father's. I do remember waiting 'till 1:00 a.m. before I started making preparations to leave. After I got a few things together, I set down to write Mom a letter. I don't remember what it said exactly but I'm sure it was nothing poetic. As I was writing it, I do remember thinking how heartbroken she was going to be when she found my bedroom empty the next morning and read my letter. I figured it was better to be a little sad now than to end up hating each other later.

My plan was simple, walk from Mom's house to Dad's and tell him I was there to stay. When I went to stay with him on the weekends, I would tell him how often and how severe the arguments were getting. He had told me on several occasions that, "you know you're welcome to stay with me if you get to where you can't take it anymore." If your parents are divorced, it is West Virginia law that when the child turns 13, he or she, can choose which parent they want to live with. I was 15 at the time and mom knew the law. She was the one who told me about it. She could have made me go back to her house until custody was changed and finalized by the court, but she also knew if she left everything alone she still had full custody of me in the eyes of court, and, therefore, final say so in the event of an emergency. When she came over to get me, or at least make sure that's where I was, she was mad, crying, and heartbroken. I felt selfish for "running away" but I knew it was for the best.

Chapter 5

High school fit me like a glove. I was popular and good at sports. It didn't take me long to figure out who was who. I started wrestling and Coach White took an immediate liking to me. Even though he was a "hard ass", he went out of his way to help me whenever he could. His wife was the gym teacher and assistant coach, but her job was to keep score and records of the matches. She also had the prettiest girls, mostly cheerleaders, as student teachers and helpers that Mrs. White recruited to be "mat girls." Mrs. White would constantly talk her wrestlers up to these girls. I had only started wrestling, but picked it up quickly. Mrs. White was constantly praising me and telling "her girls" how cute I was.

I tried to help her as much as possible when it came to getting things ready for class and putting them away. She stored most of the equipment in a little room under the bleachers. To get there you had to walk down "the tunnel" where the locker room was. One of the perks of helping Mrs. White was the interaction with those "upperclassmen" girls. They all had made comments about me being "so cute" as they called it, but it was immediately followed up with something about them being older or me being younger than them.

One day I was down in the storage room sorting things out and one of the prettiest, most popular girls Mrs. White had helping her came down to give me a hand. Billie Jo was very nice, but her "prick" boyfriend Jimmy made it difficult for me to talk to her because he was constantly picking on me. When you factor in that she was a senior and I was a freshman it wasn't like we had a lot to talk about. She would, however, compliment me openly in front of him and would even give me a little wink when she caught him not looking. I could tell right away something was different, but I couldn't put my finger on what it was. I noticed that she was getting unusually close. At one point we were face to face, maybe six inches apart staring at each other, and not saying a word. All during class I couldn't help but think that I could have kissed her if I wouldn't have been such a "chicken shit." I promised myself if I ever had another opportunity I would go for it. It didn't take long before I got that chance. At the end of class I was putting supplies away and then heading out the door when I literally ran into Billie Jo coming through the door. You know how it is when you run into someone unexpectantly and have to pull up short to keep from running into them. We were more in the storage room than the hall when our eyes locked. My heart started beating out of my chest as I went for it. I grabbed her hand to pull her farther into the storage room and out of sight before I kissed her. I was inexperienced and so nervous, I kept thinking I was doing something wrong, but when our lips touched and she started kissing me it all fell into place. We made out for a few minutes, but had to stop so we could get back to class so no one would be suspicious. She told me, "I've wanted to kiss you since the first time we met." I just made my mind up today was going to be that day." She asked me not to tell anyone, and I assured her I wouldn't.

I was about to explode by the time I got home. I knew I could tell dad my secret without him ever repeating it to anyone. As soon as I walked through the door I told him the whole story from beginning to end. I'll never forget what he said. "Do not tell anyone and never admit it even if she tells.

You never can tell what will come of it. If she and her friends know you will keep your mouth shut and/or deny it to the end, they are apt to want to do the same thing." He went on to say, "If you have to tell someone tell me, but never say anything to anyone at, near, or connected to school." That was the best advice I ever got from anyone, at any time, about anything!

When Billie found out I could keep my mouth shut, we were down there almost every day making out. As time went on she would let me do more and more. This had been going on for about three months when Mrs. White asked if I would help her and her student teachers clean out and organize the storage room. She said she would talk to my teachers to see if they could spare me for a couple days. I was thrilled and immediately said, "Yes." The two girls helping were Billie Jo and her best friend, Cindy. Cindy would only help up to lunch because she had two classes she couldn't miss. After lunch Billie Jo and I were alone. It was nice spending all day with her and really getting to interact with one another. After we had gotten everything out of the room and were about to start putting it back in order, Mrs. White came up with the idea that we paint it. Since we had it cleaned out, painting should only take a day. That was fine with me, another day of missing class, and getting to hang out with Billie Jo was right up my alley. The next morning Billie Jo, Cindy, and I started painting. By lunch we had all the room painted except for the door and a small area behind it. I came up with a brilliant idea. There was only a small path to the room, so I rearranged a few things to block us in and everyone else out. Since we had to paint behind the door and the door itself we could close the door and have a legitimate excuse why it was closed. If someone tried to enter, they would have to move a mountain of stuff to get to us and we would be able to hear them even with the door closed. Because "the tunnel" would amplify any sound or noise that was made, we knew we were safe. For an extra precaution we put all the paint, brushes, and rollers behind the door. If someone came by, we could then tell them to hold on while we moved the stuff and not to open the door or they would "spill paint everywhere." Privacy accomplished, we had sex on one of the mats. She told me repeatedly before and after that, "you better not ever tell anyone about this," and I never did with the exception of my dad.

Whenever she could get away from her "prick" boyfriend, we would have sex. We only had sex at school that one time though. It was satisfying seeing Jimmy kiss her after she had just sucked me off. I wanted so bad to ask him, 'how's my dick taste?" But somehow I resisted. Billie Jo must have told Cindy because she kept asking if I had sex with Billie Jo. When I told her, I hadn't, and she would say, "I don't know why you keep lying about it, it's ok. Billie Jo has already told me about it." I stuck to what dad told me and I denied it to the end and would occasionally throw in an, "I wish." It didn't take long before Cindy and I had the same arrangement as Billie Jo and I had. It was a sad day when graduation came along. That fall Billie Jo and Cindy both went off to college.

Chapter 6

The walk from my mother's to my father's is about five miles and like a dumbass I didn't bring a flashlight. Five miles is a long way to walk in the dark and, to make matters worse, I never passed a single car the whole way. When I left Mom's house I could see the road fairly well, because every house has at least one telephone pole in their yard with a light on it. I didn't take into account the stretches of road with no houses and the fact that the mountain I had to cross was at least two miles long from start to finish with only a single light at the very top that belongs to the state road garage. That light looked about as far away as one of the stars that was out that night. They seemed to shine extra bright, but that could have been because there was no moon to compare the brightness to. I kicked myself in the ass the whole way for not thinking to bring a flashlight.

I ran half the way because of dogs chasing after me. Most of the time I was scared and, once I got a half a mile from dads, I started running so I could get there faster and the whole thing would be over. When I got there my father wasn't home so I sat up and waited for him. It was a little after 4:00 a.m. before he got home. Needless to say he was surprised to see me. With one look, he knew I was there to stay. It turned out to be the best decision I ever made.

Dad's house was small and cozy with only one bedroom. I was allowed to do pretty much what I wanted as long as I wasn't acting stupid. I still had practice of one kind or another, and by the time I got home I just wanted to hang out with my dad. Sometimes he would be waiting for me to go fishing or playing cards with my uncles on Mamaw's porch. Dad always had a few dollars to give me so I could join in. We mostly played quarter limit seven card stud. I won more than I lost, which was an accomplishment in itself considering I was playing against grown men. Sometimes we would go to my Uncle James' house to shoot basketball.

I didn't play basketball in high school, I wrestled. I did, however, become good friends with our new basketball coach. He was a young guy- straight out of college and wild as a buck. He had a good sense of humor and was quick with a smile that reached from ear to ear. Andrew loved basketball and anything connected with it. I've never seen anyone so passionate about anything. When he would start talking about anything related to basketball, his voice became more animated and his face would shine like he was on the verge of crying. He wanted me to play for him and constantly tried to get me to switch sports.

I wasn't old enough to drive yet and because I was in a different county than where I went to school, there were no buses for me to ride. My father had to get up and take me to school just like Mom had always done. Andrew lived about a mile away and offered to take me to school which kept Dad from having to take me. So Dad was all for it. Andrew would drive out of his way every morning to pick me up without fail.

Every summer he would go to various basketball camps along the east coast to be an instructor. Whenever he got back from camp, he came baring gifts. He would bring college jerseys, shorts, hats, and anything else he could get his hands on. He gave stuff away to all his friends, but he made sure I got the good stuff. He gave me shorts and jerseys the players themselves gave him.

By this time I was smoking pot everyday- especially in the morning. If I was late getting up and didn't have time to smoke at the house before we left, I would smoke in the car on our way to school. Andrew would hang half his body out of the window like Jim Carey did in the beginning of the movie, "Ace Ventura," when he had his windshield beat in with a baseball bat. He told me he did this because, "that fucking smell sticks to me like glue and you know every morning I have to go in the office and check my box."

Because basketball and wrestling season started and ended about the same time, I couldn't play basketball. When neither of us had practice he would take me home in the evenings. On Fridays we would go the liquor store and he would buy a fifth of Crown Royal. As soon as he had the chance he would throw the lid away. He was notorious for shooting beer lids out the window by snapping his fingers with the lid resting on his thumb. He had a good aim. I remember one time on the way back home he told me, "Roll your window down." I didn't think anything of it. I figured he was shooting another beer cap out the window. When I saw it was the lid to the liquor bottle, I didn't know what to think. "Why in the fuck did you do that for?" I asked. He said with a big shit eating grin on his face, "we don't need a lid if we're drinking it." He was a mess and I loved him to death for it.

It wasn't long before he was involved with one of the girls at school. I had told him about walking in on my art teacher having sex with a student in his supply closet during lunch. Maybe that gave him an idea or planted an unintentional seed about having a romantic relationship with students. It wasn't long before she was sneaking into his class room a couple times a week during lunch. He got so loose with the whole thing that he was taking the school's audio visual equipment and making amateur porn in his class room during these lunch time rendezvous. He would sometimes show me bits and pieces of them and I could see why he was so crazy about her. Everyone knew they were a couple. After a while, they did very little to hide it.

Dad bought me an old dodge pickup truck and I worked on it every day the summer after I turned 16 and made my license. While I was turning bolts, my friends were running around in their new cars; it made me work that much harder to get my truck on the road. My father was a fairly good mechanic and I had been helping him for a few years. When it came to working on my truck he only helped enough to get his hands dirty. He would tell me, "this is your baby", and walk off after pointing to what I had to take off. He would also tell me, "come and get me when you're finished and I'll make sure you put everything back together right. I may want to borrow it to go the store sometime and I don't want it breaking down on me." Mom bought an engine and other parts and dad got it painted. By the time football season started my junior year, I had a ride.

It wasn't long before I got my first serious girlfriend. Her name was Crystal and she was the first girl I ever loved. I was three years older than her, but she was very mature. Our father's knew each other and dad told me several times, "you better watch yourself as far as that girl goes. Billy is crazy as hell." Billy turned out to be friendly and very funny. I still minded what I said and did around him though. I did, however, sneak her out of her bedroom window almost every night. She would sometimes off set her mattress so there would be a gap against her wall. I would sleep on her box spring in the little cubby hole she had made. That way if her dad or step mother came in I was hidden.

Sometimes I wouldn't get home until 3:00 or 4:00 a.m. Since I had to pass Andrew's house on the way back home, I would stop in if I saw a light on. At least two times a week he would have four or five guys over playing drinking games. He would drink, smoke, and party all night, but when 5:00 came he stopped drinking and ran everyone off. That way by the time 8:00 a.m. rolled around he would be sober enough to go to work. Even though he may have felt like shit.

The ticket booth that was used for football games was right beside Andrew's classroom and for a long time it was my personal smoking booth. My buddies and I would meet there at lunch to smoke a bowl or joint. I only had one or two friends that I smoked with at school. I was heavily involved in sports and if any of my coaches found out they may have kicked me off the team. They may have had their suspicions, but nothing more. Dad had started selling a little pot to his friends, so my supply didn't run out very often. This also kept me from running around looking for it and doing god knows what. This actually reduced my chances of getting into trouble, because if I wasn't at practice I was with Dad fishing, playing cards, or hanging out getting high.

When summer vacation came around Andrew and I would run around, play basketball, and drink beer. That was, whenever my father and I wasn't fishing or riding around ourselves. Most of the time we ended up at the pool because it was hard not to find a game down there. Andrew's girlfriend would also show up, but she would go inside and swim while we played ball. If they talked at all it would be through me. Sometimes I would talk to her while Andrew acted like he was waiting on me to finish, but it would be really them that carried on the conversation. He would keep these talks brief though- no more than a minute tops. That was the only type of contact they had in the open, and since I was almost always with him, it didn't look too suspicious. More and more people found out and started talking until eventually it was common knowledge what was going on. Everyone liked Andrew; he acted, and talked like he was still in high school himself even though he was twenty two. I think his "girlfriend" was sixteen or seventeen, so it's not like the age difference was that big. I knew several girls in high school dating guys twenty- two and twenty- three year olds, but none of them were our teacher. As their feelings for one another grew so did their bravery. He truly loved this girl and she him, but like all good things, it came to an end.

We were at the pool playing ball and he told me they had been fighting. I saw her car pull in and I knew it was her. He didn't try to hide anymore; he walked straight up to her as she was getting out of the car. It was a big parking lot so he had to walk a long ways before he reached her, and I was on his heels trying to rein him in, but he wasn't listening to anything I said. He was focused on her. I tried to keep up with him to try and camouflage things the best I could. As soon as he got within talking distance, they started yelling and cussing each other. I gave up trying to conceal them fighting. A blind man could have seen what was going on. She went to walk off and he caught her arm to stop her. He couldn't have gotten more attention if he pulled a gun on her. She pulled away again and he followed her until she got to the entrance of the pool. When she went in we left. He never said a word the whole way home. He knew he had fucked up.

The school learned what had happened and basically forced him to resign. Andrew, being Andrew, did me one last solid before he left. He gave me the key to his private bathroom. Actually it was the girl's bathroom during football games, but it was kept locked the rest of the time. It was very clean and fairly large. It had six stalls, four sinks, and a large mirror. Andrew would let the cheerleaders store mats in there. He could never say no and it wasn't long before it was full of their belongings. The only people in the entire school who had a key were the janitor and me. The janitor couldn't find the key half the time, because his key ring was so full of keys.

After Andrew resigned I went there often. Sometimes I would go to smoke up, other times I would bring a girl for a lunch time quickie. More often than not, it was both. I kept the key in the same place I kept the apartment key when I was younger, through my shoe lace. That was a tried and true method, and I knew if I lost it there was no replacement to be had. To unlock the door I would simply slip off my shoe. It wasn't long before the girls started talking, but when they asked me about this girl, or that one, I would deny it. Some of the girls took offense to me not telling and backed up their side of the story by telling about the key being on my shoe lace. Other girls would ask, "What's that key go to," being either jealous, curious, or a smartass. Sometimes I would ask in return, "Do you want to find out," and a lot said, "Yes!" While the guys asked, "Can I use your spot?" It was almost always backed up by some sad story, but I only let one person borrow it one time, and that was my cousin Kenneth.

    One day I was down there making out with this girl when we heard the principal and janitors voice along with keys being searched for, and inserted into the lock. It scared the hell out of us, she asked, "what are we going to do?" I went to the only stall that had a window in it and we both jumped out. I had barely gotten the window shut before they came in. After that I never felt comfortable down there again and because everyone knew about "the key" being on my shoe I took it off. Whenever I was asked about it I would tell them "I lost it" which I eventually did.

Chapter 7

Throughout high school I was not very faithful to Crystal. Not because of her, but because we went to different schools. I imagine it had a lot to do with my raging teenage hormones as well.

The summer before I started college was never boring. I was always busy doing something and had people stopping by the house all the time. It was late one night when one of my friends stopped in and said, "I got this girl that wants to have sex with two guys. Get ready and you can go with me to pick her up." I told him, "It's late and I'm not going to cheat on Crystal anymore, I've turned over a new leaf." He turned and threw a "will see" over his shoulder as he went out the door. Dad hadn't got back from the club yet and I was on the verge of going to sleep, when my buddy came through the door with this beautiful girl with jet black hair. She had all the curves in all the right places, and once I started to talking to her, I was surprised when I found out she was very nice and funny. We all set around getting high and it didn't take long for one thing to lead to another and we both ended up sleeping with her.

I felt miserable for cheating on Crystal again, and swore if I got by with it this "one last time" I would never cheat on her again. I thought I might have had a good chance of Crystal not finding out, because they went to different schools in different counties. Of course, I had no such luck. That girl must have had Crystal on speed dial. The very next day she was asking me about it. She found out in less than

24 hours, and of course, I denied it. This went on for about a month before I was basically tricked into telling on myself.

I was at my friend Jordan's house and was getting ready to go 4-wheeling when Crystal called accusing me of sleeping with that girl again. She wanted me to confront her, but I didn't want any part of it. She said, "I have her phone number, call her and tell her to call me and tell me you never slept with her." I told her, "I'm not calling her or anyone else. If I had her number that would be something else for you to bitch about." Somehow she talked me into agreeing to have the girl call me. I was ready to do whatever it was going to take to put the whole thing behind me. Jordan was trying to get me to hurry up, but in a few minutes the girl called me. I told her that I had fun, but I made a mistake. I went on to explain how much I loved Crystal and asked that she tell her nothing happened. I made it clear that I had already told her 100 times, but she doesn't believe me. She said, "What do you want me to say?" And I responded with, "anything but the truth." No sooner than I said that I heard another voice, a very familiar voice! It was Crystal and all I could make out before I hung up was her screaming, "and what's the truth you son of a bitch?" My heart dropped. I had been tricked. Crystal was on a three way call and I didn't know it. I felt like a complete and utter asshole, that's not to mention the embarrassment of getting caught in a lie.

I waited for over a month hoping she would have calmed down a little before I started calling her again. Even then it took several weeks of begging and pleading before she reluctantly took me back. I swore to her and made a vow to myself that I would never be unfaithful to her again. I would never cheat on her or anyone else as long as I lived. We were together a few months and were getting along beautifully when my resolve was put to the test. I stopped off at Jordan's house on my way to Crystal's to see what he was going to get into later that night. That was the routine. We would go out with our girlfriends and meet up afterwards to drink a few beers and get high. I had stayed at Jordan's house on a regular basis growing up and I had a huge crush on his older sister. Jordan and I made plans to meet later that night and as I was leaving, his sister stopped me to say hello. I could tell she was a little friendlier than usual, and the subject of her finding someone to go out with came up. I had made several suggestions, all of which she turned down. She made a comment, "I want to go out with someone more like you." For a second I was speechless. I finally had my chance to take her out, but I made up my mind not to cheat on Crystal again no matter who it was with. So I played stupid and went off to pick up Crystal.

Soon after that my father had his car accident. Things were never the same, but Crystal was terrific. She was loving, kind, and very understanding. I was devastated and if it hadn't been for her and the rest of my family and friends, God only knows what I may have done. This cemented our relationship. I knew then I had someone truly special.

One night I was on my way to see her, but about half way to her house I ran into her and one of her friends. I pulled over, and got out to check and make sure her friend was ok to drive. The way she was driving I thought she was drunk. Swerving, flashing her lights, blowing her horn, and speeding. She was normally a good driver who obeyed the traffic laws, but on this day that wasn't the case. You have to keep in mind Crystal was only 15 at the time. She got out of the car to meet me and said, "We need to talk, I've got something to tell you." We went back to my truck and that's when she dropped the bomb on me. She was pregnant! I was floored, but I told myself not to panic because if I did she would too. I told her that I loved her and that "we're in this together, and I'll do anything you ask or want me to do. We'll figure this out; you know how much I love you." She started crying as she buried her head on my shoulder. I had noticed her friend hadn't left yet, so I told Crystal to go and tell her that she was ok and I was going to take her home. She started crying again and said, "You can't, Dad said he would kill you if he saw you. That's why we came to find you before you showed up at my house." I guess that explains the reason why they were acting and driving like they were. Now on top of being scared and not knowing what to do. I've got to look out for her crazy dad who I'd already been warned to be careful around. I couldn't blame him; she was only 15 and had her whole life ahead of her.

I avoided her house. The only time we got to talk is when she could sneak and call me. This went on for a few weeks and I was feeling like a bitch for not going to talk to her dad, but every time I mentioned it she would beg me not to. The drive to and from school was about an hour and a half each way on some of the most country mountain roads you could imagine. It was hilly, curvy, narrow, and most of it didn't even have lines on it. I would drive for miles without passing a car or house. I had plenty of time to think. I finally made up my mind to stop off and talk to Billy. I figured I had to face him sooner or later and I was tired of feeling helpless. If I was man enough to make a baby, I would be man enough to take responsibility for it. If he was going to kill me, then so be it, but it was coming to some kind of conclusion. I couldn't bear not seeing or speaking to Crystal anymore. Before I started off on the drive back home, I told my cousin Jessie of my intentions and got a six-pack to help boost my courage. Jessie wished me luck and told me, "If you're not dead call me and tell me how it went." I rehearsed what I was going to say the whole way there. I can't describe how scared I was when I pulled into Crystal's driveway. I expected Billy to come out shooting, but he never did. I was walking up the step of the porch when Crystal's step mom just so happened to be coming out. She looked at me like, what the hell are you doing here? She was nice and took pity on me though. I think it was because she understood what I was going through. She was only a year or so older than me and had two children of her own. I told her I was there to talk to Billy and she said, "I'll go get him." He came out and sat down on the swing and before he had a chance to say anything I began to plea my case. I told him, "I love her with all my heart and even though I don't make much money, I'll quit school and get another job if I have to." It was a while before he said anything. Well, it could have been only a few seconds but it seemed like forever. The pause before he spoke made me nervous and a little scared. When he finally spoke he said, "Well you're more of a man than I thought. You're welcome at my house anytime." I went on to let him know there were no lengths I wasn't willing to go to, to provide for Crystal and our baby. I asked if he had any advice and he said, "My advice would have been not to get her pregnant, but it's too late for that." Billy was a hard man to figure out, but I never had any problems or disagreement with him. I asked him if I could go pick her up from cheerleading practice and to tell her about everything, and so she could tell me exactly what was going on with her. The only time I got to talk to her was when she could sneak and call me which was not very often. He was more than happy to let me pick her up so he wouldn't have to. Billy didn't like to leave the house unless it was absolutely necessary.

When I pulled in the parking lot and she saw me she came running out. She gave me a kiss saying, "You know Dad's going to kill you if he sees you?" She didn't know what to say when I told her that I had already spoke to her father and he and I had come to an understanding. I asked her, "Who do you think told me it was ok to pick you up?"

After that things were great. I went to school during the day and worked all night. Anytime I wasn't doing either of those, I was sleeping at Crystal's. She would cook for me before I went to work. I could stop in at her house on my way to work and leave from there. That was about the only time I got to spend with her during the week. I kept telling myself that I needed to marry her. Not because she was pregnant, but because I loved her that much. She was all I could ever want and ask for. By the time I made up my mind to ask her and started saving money for a ring, everything went to hell.

The coal mine where I worked shut down because of high sulfur content in the coal. Crystal kept bringing up abortion and the fact that I didn't have a job. I could see where she was coming from. After all, she was only 15. A lot of it also came from her mother, who I knew was only trying to help. I told her I would support her in whatever decision she made. Deep down I think I wanted her to have the child, but maybe neither of us was ready to be parents. I'm sure it was probably the best thing for her. Sixteen with a baby is a hard road to travel: even if I did everything that was required of me. If I would have had to quit school work two jobs, I would have done it, no question asked. She went ahead with the abortion. The abortion didn't change our relationship though, if anything it made us closer. Because of sports injuries, I had become familiar with pain medication in high school. I was only taking medication when absolutely necessary and was really in pain. I did, however, liked the way it made me feel. I don't know if it was the fact that she was constantly around me and my friends who were taking pills or because of the abortion that she started experimenting. On a rare occasion, she would take a hit off a joint.

Her grandparents were good, honest, God fearing people. They were constantly asking us to go to church with them. We finally agreed and Sunday we met at her grandmother's house before we went. Her great- grandmother asked us to ride with her, so that's what we did. Her great- grandmother had an uncommon energy and spirit about her. She was constantly moving around, busy doing this or that.

When we got there everyone was warm and welcoming. They all said hello and told us how glad they were we came. I don't think I ever met a nicer group of people. The building wasn't very old, although it had an unmistakable feeling to it: like it had a history. Everything was nice and clean, but not over the top or flashy. When the preacher started preaching it seemed like every word he said was directed towards Crystal and me. He was simply stating the facts as I had known them to be. He was honest, sincere, and was glowing as he poured his heart out. I was very touched by his words but Crystal more so, because when alter call came she went to repent. As she was praying and asking God for forgiveness, I walked out heartbroken and confused. I knew I had lost her forever, but who was I to try and stand between her and salvation. Since I had rode with Crystal's great-grandmother my truck was about 3 miles away at her house, so I took off walking to get it. On my way the preacher's words kept repeating themselves in my head, before I knew it I had tears running down my face. It wasn't long before someone stopped and gave me a ride. I got in my pick-up and had every intention of driving home, but once I got to the turn off that took me home, I didn't make it. Before I knew it I was back in the church parking lot. Crystal, her great-grandmother, the preacher, and his wife were standing outside talking. I got out and as I approached them the preacher looked at me and said, "God has touched your heart and it's scared you hasn't it?" He knew his words had touched me. I was running, not from God, but because I didn't know if I could stop the things I was doing and live the life I was supposed to. When I left the church for the second time, my sins were forgiven and I was saved.

It was a difficult change of pace and lifestyle from what I was used to. I quit all drug use, smoking cigarettes, hanging out in places with friends who were not conducive to my new lifestyle. The church and its members welcomed Crystal and me with open arms. They did all they could to help teach us the things we needed to know as it pertained to our newly found salvation. Even harder than adjusting to no more drug use was no more sex. Needless to say, Crystal's resolve was much stronger than my own. I came to the conclusion that for Crystal and me to work, we needed to get married. When I asked Crystal to marry me, I didn't get the "yes" I expected. In its place I got a, "I'll have to ask the preacher and see what he says." I was shocked and didn't feel the same towards her after that. We did, however, talk to the preacher and his wife. They both thought it was a good idea taking into account our circumstances, but warned us to be careful.

Crystal quit cheerleading and immersed herself into the church and church activities. It was a daily struggle for me to honor the vows and promises I had made to God. If it wasn't for Crystal and the fear of losing her, I wouldn't have lasted as long as I did. For six months I fought a good fight until I just became overwhelmed. One of the people I went to church with gave me a job surveying. The guy I was partnered to work with was not the best influence. Not to say it took much of an influence to start back down that old familiar road. We would smoke pot and occasionally do a pill or two and it wasn't long before I had lost control. I started doing more and more drugs. Eventually I quit my job and left the church. I stuck around a while half- heartedly going through the motions, but I wasn't fooling anyone. It was clear that I wasn't the same person.

The defining moment came when it was time to go the annual church camp meeting which was held every year over the 4th of July weekend. Crystal and I were on and off at this point and the only reason why I was willing to go was to appease her. Crystal and most of the others left a few days before I was planning to leave. The day before I was supposed to leave I decided to go to the beach instead. I had just bought a corvette and thought I would have more fun at the beach showing off my new car. Plus, I would have only been going through the motions and lying to everyone if I would have gone to the church's annual get together.

I went to the beach and had a pretty good time, although my mind was constantly drifting back to Crystal. I met up with a couple friends down there. One guy who wasn't all that good of a friend had a pretty little girlfriend. Her name was Laura. Every chance we had we would talk and flirt with one another. Even though I considered her boyfriend a friend, he was still a smug bastard that acted like he was better than everyone else. So if I had the chance to take his pretty soft- spoken girlfriend, then more power to me.

As I would later learn Crystal met her future husband at this same time. From what I heard he is a very nice hard-working person. They had at least one child together and they now live in or around Washington D.C.

Chapter 8

The summer before I started college my cousin, Jessie, helped me get a job at the local coal mine where he worked. I was hired to work all weekend starting at 7:00 a.m. Saturday morning and work forty continuous hours until 11:00 p.m. Sunday night. Jessie would then start his shift. Jessie and I went to the same school so it only made sense for us to ride together and share the cost of the drive. I felt sorry for him after seeing him come dragging in after working all night. He has green and hazel colored eyes and when he went without sleep his eyes would water nonstop. I couldn't help but feel sorry for him.

Jessie had been at the mine for over a year before I started working there, and was never given a raise. I started out making the same thing he was making even though he had been there longer. We both made $152.00 a week after taxes, for a forty hour week. The forty continuous hours on the weekend was a much better shift than working five days a week eight hours a day. I started doing more than I was required to do strictly out of boredom. Our responsibilities were the same; the only difference was Jessie had to do them every night, instead of only once on the weekend like I did. All the extra work I was doing must have impressed the boss because he switched mine and Jessie's shifts. Jessie was as happy as he could be with the switch. He could finally get some much needed rest. He had been trying for a while to get moved back to weekends. After the switch it didn't take me long to figure out why Jessie looked so tired. It's because he was. It wasn't long before working every day and going to school was whipping my ass as well.

I didn't get off of work until 7:00 a.m. and was twenty minutes away from my mother's house, if I didn't run into any traffic and broke the speed limit the whole way. I was initially going to Dad's house to get ready, but it took an extra ten minutes and that put me and Jessie ten minutes late for class. So, I started getting ready at her house to save an extra ten minutes every morning. Even if everything went smoothly it was still a race trying to get to class by 9:00 every morning.

The next semester Jessie and I went to school on different days and at different times so we rarely rode together. The boss tried keeping me later and later every morning no matter how many times I told him I had to leave or I was going to be late for class. I was late at least twice a week. I was never more than five minutes late, but late was late in the professor's eyes. He had a policy that allowed us to miss only three classes each semester and three tardies was the equivalent to one absence. I was close to going over the three days that was allotted us. The professor asked me to stay after class to express his concerns about my tardies. He asked, "What do we have to do to get you here on time?" I explained to him that I had to work just to be able to afford to come to class every day and told him what my job consisted of. I told him why I was late and no matter what I did sometimes it couldn't be helped. He asked, "Can't you come straight from work instead of going home first?" I told him I could, but I would be filthy. He asked me, "Would you rather come to class dirty or be dismissed because of too many missed days?" I told him that I would be there bright and early the next morning.

I was the first one in class the next morning and just as I said, I was filthy. I was even a little wet from setting pumps the night before. I didn't wash my face or change my boots. I only washed my hands so I wouldn't get coal dirt all over my steering wheel. After class the teacher said, "You weren't kidding about being filthy." You could see coal dirt in the chair when I got up to leave. After the 9:00 a.m. class I had an hour break before my next class. I would take that time to go into the bathroom and wash my face. I'll never forget leaving class that first day. Every step I took left a perfect coal dirt outline of the sole of my boot on the carpet. I could track myself where ever I went. My friends thought it was hilarious. They said the professor thought I was lying about working in the coal mines and that being the reason for my lateness. It took a few more days before the professor called me back into his office. This time he was whistling a different tune. He said, "The janitor is on my ass over all the coal dirt and boot prints you've been leaving everywhere." He went on to say, "If you promise not to be any later than you were before, I would prefer it if you would come to class bathed."

After school I would go to Dad's house to get some sleep before work. It didn't matter who was there or what they were doing, Dad would run them off so I wouldn't be disturbed. As they were going out the door he would brag to them about "my boy" going to school all day and working all night. He told everyone he saw that and most of the time end it with, "that's my hero right there." I loved knowing I was making dad proud. Mom expected nothing less, but that's not to say that she wasn't just as proud as he was. Dad just had a unique way of expressing it.

I would have him wake me up by 7:00 p.m. so I could stop by my girlfriend Crystal's house before I went to work. Sometimes she would cook for me, if she didn't get to save me a plate from supper. During the days when I didn't have class or a later class I would stop by and she would make me breakfast.

After a while school and work started taking its toll. I was falling behind in my school work and could never get enough sleep. I hated going to work and crawling back into that hole to set pumps night after night. It should have been illegal to have a mine with an average height of twenty eight inches. The sad thing was there were dozens more that were just as low. It came as a relief when I found out the mine was shutting down because of "high sulfur coal." I was there for over a year and never missed a day's work and haven't missed working there a day since.

Chapter 9

I was awoken by a knock at the door early in the morning of May 31st, 1997. I thought I had accidently locked Dad out of the house again. So when I opened the door I was surprised to see my uncles and cousin standing there. First thing that went through my mind was fishing trip. That thought only lasted a moment, because I could see by the looks on their faces something was wrong. They told me that dad had been in a serious car accident. As I was putting on my clothes and getting ready, I questioned them about what they knew and what hospital he was in. That's when they told me Dad had been killed. I didn't believe that for one second. Hurt maybe, dead, never! My father went through cars like most people did sunglasses: about two or three every summer. I have seen him come through car wrecks that tore his whole eye lid off to the point of where his eye was lying on his cheek. He and Uncle Jeff were hit by a car in front of our house and Jeff died from his wounds, but Dad walked down the hill and some fifty plus steps to the house. He did that with one side of his ribcage crushed, a punctured lung, and more cuts than I cared to count. When he sat down at the kitchen table and I started trying to stop the bleeding there was at least a quart of blood pooled under the chair he was sitting in. He survived all that! No one could make me believe he had been killed in a car accident; I didn't even want to hear it. Just another car wreck where someone had seen the car and said, "There is no way anyone could have survived that." They were wrong every time. This was just another example of someone else jumping to conclusions. We had gotten these calls in the past and Dad would be sitting on the couch watching TV. I would tell him,

"I don't know if you know it or not, but you were killed in that car wreck." It was a never ending bad joke.

When we were walking out the door, I noticed Dad's car was in its usual spot but mine was gone. My car was a beautiful red '73 Camaro that I had built from the frame up with the money I had gotten for graduation. Dad had given me a very powerful 400 small block engine. That was one of the reasons why I bought the car to begin with. I knew I could get that engine if I had a car to put it in. The day before I had given the car a complete tune-up and oil change so it was running beautifully. I was kind of pissed off when I saw my car gone, but I knew why he had taken it. The knowledge of my car not in its spot made a car accident more likely, but still couldn't fathom that he had been killed. Never-the-less we had to go check. If dad had been taken to the hospital he may need a ride home. The fire department knew the general area where the accident occurred. They told us there was a single car accident near the football field, but didn't know who it was or the extent of their injuries. I told my uncles while on our way to the field, "if there was a fatality they would have known and told us." To this they gave no response. They only looked at one another with the same grave expression. The closer we got the more nervous I became. There was constant speculation about how he had wrecked after we found out the exact location. In front of the football field there is a hump and if you went over it too fast it felt like you were leaving the ground. Everything was starting to add up. He was flying because the car was running exceptionally well, hit the little hump too fast and went airborne. The one thing that didn't make sense was what he was doing down that way to begin with. The only thing we could figure is that he was taking some girl home.

Once we got close to the football field we could see the traffic was backed up and people were out of their cars talking. We drove around the traffic as far as we could and pulled off at the tennis courts that were beside the football field. We got within sixty or seventy yards of the accident. I could see the back end of my car. It stuck out like a sore thumb, because of its bright red color. Not to mention it was cut in half: T-boned against a guardrail with the back end stuck straight in the air. It was a mangled mess. The front end was completely detached from the rest of the car. I mean from the windshield up. The motor, transmission, and the whole front clip were 150 feet away. It was then that I realized the severity of it all. Before my uncle could stop I jumped out and was running toward what was left of my car. Once I saw the wreckage the only thought I had was finding Dad and praying he was alive. Deep down I knew for once the rumors were true. As I got closer I could make out a body lying next to what was once a car. There were people standing around and walking up to the body to take a look like it was a freak show. It was reminiscent of how outlaws were displayed once they were shot and killed in the old west. Before I could reach him I was stopped and held by a state trooper. I tried to make the dumb, son of a bitch understand that was my father and I had more of a right there than he did. I will never forget his emotionless expression, cold, uncaring attitude and his voice as he told me, "He's dead there is nothing you can do for him." By this time my uncles had caught up with me and told the cop, "Get your fucking hands off of him!" They had heard what he had said as they were drawing closer to me. If he wouldn't have let me go when he did, there would not have been a second request. My family doesn't repeat themselves very often and this was one of those times. They try to obey the law for the most part, but when it comes to family and standing up for what they think is right, the law and the police can be damned. One of my uncles put his arm around my shoulder and led me back to the car. It felt like the world and everything in it had stopped. I could only hear my uncle demanding, "Cover him up, this is not a Goddamn peepshow." Then my ears started ringing and everything went silent, I started feeling dizzy, weak, and sick to my stomach as it finally hit me. I will never see my father again! I collapsed and started crying. My whole world was over and it felt like my soul was being ripped out through my throat.

On the way back home one of my uncles learned my Dad's friend, Eric, was with him and was in critical condition, but looked as if he was going to make it. He was taking Eric home. That was the reason he was down that way. I can't begin to put in words the heartache I felt. It was like the whole world went dark. It is the only time I have ever felt hopeless. I couldn't stand to be awake. At least if I was sleeping I didn't have to deal with reality or feel the pain. Dad use to tell me whenever he thought I was going to do something that I could get hurt doing, "Be careful if anything was to happen to you I wouldn't be able to stand it." I know what he meant and believed him. His brother's death weighed heavy on his heart and I was his only comfort. He told me his darkest secrets and I have never told any of them to anyone. I remembered what he said and took it into account every time I did something risky. It never occurred to me to question if I would "be able to stand it" if something happened to him. It was almost too much pain for me to bear. My best friend and my father gone forever!

I would wake up and drink myself back into a coma every day. Sometimes I had the help of Xanax which was prescribed to me for anxiety. They would put me out quick. As soon as I came back to, I would do it again and again and again. Before long I couldn't get any peace even while I slept. The pain and heartache, along with the images I saw that day, started invading my dreams. I struggled for a long time trying to fight through it. I would tell myself, "Man up, you can take it, don't let this beat you." I had a hard time, mostly because everything I saw reminded me of my father. My heart overflowing with grief and felt like it was ready to explode. I would just start crying out of nowhere. The grief built up until it had no place to go and came pouring out of me with no warning.

One of the main reasons, other than the magnitude of losing my father, was I felt responsible in contributing to the factors surrounding his death. The day before his accident, I borrowed his car to go the pool to meet Crystal. The insurance had run out on my car or I would have taken it. On the way to the pool Dad's car started overheating. Instead of pulling off the road and letting it cool down like I knew I was supposed to do, I kept going thinking it could cool down once I got to the pool. I made it to the pool, but the car had gotten so hot that I could hear water boiling in the overflow when I got out. On the way home I made it a little over half way before I had to stop, let it cool down and add water to the radiator. I never said anything to Dad about the car overheating. I could only hope that I didn't let it get so hot that the engine blew a head gasket. When I got back I still had to finish tuning my car. I had already put wires, distributing cap, rotary button, and changed the oil before I left. All I had to do was change the spark plugs. After I got it all put back together I took it down the road for a test drive.

It's hard to believe how much a tune-up can improve a car's performance. When I came back I put my tools away and was walking up the bottom when I realized I had the car keys in my hand. This was very odd because I would always leave my keys in the car because I was so prone to losing them. I put them in my pocket and took maybe two steps before I decided to go back and put them in the car.

It was my fault Dad's car kept overheating. All I had to do was stop, let the car cool down, and put some water in the radiator. If I would have only done that Dad wouldn't have had any reason to stop and trade cars. Even if I had not walked back down the bottom and put the keys in the car, things may have turned out differently. If I would have had them with me he would have had to wake me up to get them. If that happened I may have been able to talk him into letting me drive or I could have simply acted like I had lost them.

A couple days after the wreck I went to see Eric in the hospital. He had extensive injuries, but he was going to survive. I also had feelings of regret and responsibility for the shape he was in. I couldn't hold back my grief and sorrow, I wept uncontrollably. It took me a few minutes before I was able to swallow it back down.

The funeral was a blur. I was heavily medicated and drunk on alcohol, but mostly on sorrow. I can only recall seeing him lying there, so cold, and alone. Even now it's hard for me to pull an image of him out of my head without seeing him lying in that coffin.

I was in a drunken stupor for several months after my father's death. I quit going to school all together. If it wasn't for my mother, family, and friends, I don't think I could have made it. Especially Crystal, she was one of the few people I could stand to be around for any length of time. She would set with me for hours and we never had to say a word. The only time I was awake and not in total misery was when we were together, not speaking a word to one another. As long as I didn't speak, the sorrow was at a minimum.

My father's friends would come by to see how I was doing. They would try to comfort me in any way they could. Once Eric got to moving around he came up and told me about the whole thing from beginning to end. Although it wasn't without much prompting on my part. He mostly confirmed what I already knew. They stopped to get my car because Dad's was overheating. They were going well over 100 mph when he came over that hump at the football field. What he said was, "We went airborne and when we came back down we landed in the ditch line. Charles about had us straightened back out, but we hit that second little rise and there was no saving us then. We crossed completely up and the last thing I remember is seeing that guardrail right before we hit. Next thing I knew I'm waking up in the hospital." He also said that he was approached by an attorney about suing Dad's insurance. When Eric told him there was no insurance on the car, he said he could sue my father's estate. Eric told me not to worry that he would never do that to me; that I had already lost too much. "Plus Charles was my friend." He was as good as his word. He never tried to sue or ask me for anything, even though I'm sure he could have taken everything Dad and I had.

Chapter 10

Dad had been selling a little pot at the time of his death. I knew he had some put away somewhere. The only thing was I had to find it. I didn't exactly know where it was, but once I began looking for it, it wasn't long before I found it. It wasn't a whole lot, but to me it was a substantial amount. Dad had taken the trouble of weighing it out in ounces and what I found was 12 bags. So I took over the family business with a 12 oz. head start. I knew he had gotten it on a front (credit). I also knew whom he had gotten it from. At first Dad's friends would stop by to see how I was doing, but gradually they quit coming around except for a handful of them. Dad once told me, "If you can count your friends on more than one hand you're either lying to yourself or you're being lied to." Even though my father wasn't an educated man, he knew people and we'll say the "streets" for lack of a more appropriate word.

I live in the country where there are no cities or streets. What we do have are towns, roads, and hollows. We don't wear our pants down past our ass nor do we feel tough because we have a gun. Everyone has a gun in the country and usually before they are 10 years old. For the most part we handle the disputes that can't be talked out or reasoned to satisfaction the old fashion way. Through the tried and true method of a fist fight. It may seem barbaric, but nine out of ten fights both parties leave feeling satisfied that the problem has been resolved. For my taste it beats arguing and airing your dirty laundry to everyone, degrading one another to any and all who will listen. It also beats the hell out of shooting each other. How many times has either of those options produced a solution that left both parties content or satisfied?

Out of the handful of Dad's friends who were truly his friends and cared about my well-being, two stuck out. Their names were Andy and Donnie Roberts. They were brothers and had been lifelong friends of my father. They had known one another as children and they both took a special interest in me. They took me under their wing and probably kept me from going to prison. Andy is who my father got the marijuana from, and whom I now owed, for the 12 oz. of pot that he had never been paid for and never once asked about the money or weed. I had to bring it up to him and all he said was, "Don't worry about it." I told him I had been selling a little of it and he gave me some advice and opinions on who to and who not to sell to. I had paid attention to dad and how he handled and dealt with everything surrounding any kind of hustle, especially when it came to selling pot.

I decided to go back to school the following semester. It wasn't so much that I wanted to go, but because I knew that was what dad would have wanted. Mom, family, girlfriend, Andy, and Donnie were all very vocal and encouraging. They were all constantly asking me when I was going back to school or if I had enrolled yet? They would tell me how proud dad was and how he was always bragging about me to everyone. Eventually I gave in and went back. I found it was much easier than I thought. A lot of it had to do with being able to concentrate on something other than Dad's death. I immersed myself in my studies and because I didn't have to work to pay for the expenses to and from school, I was better rested and actually had time to study and do assignments. My grades improved and I never missed a class or was late.

Everything was going great. So I should have expected "Murphy's Law" to kick in. I was told by Crystal that she and I were going to be parents. I have to admit at first I didn't want anything to do with a baby, but that was mostly the initial shock of it all. I knew I wasn't making enough money to support Crystal and a child. That's when I took my level of hustling to the point of trying to make serious money. Before I had only done what I had to do to get by. Now, I was worrying about tomorrow and made up my mind to make every dollar I possibly could. I told myself I was going to be the best father I could possibly be. I also knew having a child was expensive. Crystal had told me that her mother wanted her to have an abortion, but I didn't think she was seriously considering it.

I was setting in my truck between classes one day and had forgotten to bring anything to smoke. I had two hours to kill before my next class. I decided to simply ask the first person I saw that I knew got high if they had a joint they would sell or smoke with me. I knew enough pot heads to know one when I saw one. I watched as the next group of classes let out and right off the bat I struck gold. Here comes this guy walking straight to me that was wearing a tie dyed shirt, blue jeans with the biggest legs I have ever seen cut off at the bottom so they wouldn't drag the ground, with sandals on. I knew without a shadow of a doubt that this guy got high. I walked up to him and introduced myself and started explaining my dilemma. He felt my pain and introduced himself as Pete. I was told to follow him to his car. Once we sat down he produced a gigantic glass pipe that was as colorful as the shirt he was wearing and proceeded to load it with some of the best pot I ever smoked. I had met my first hippie.

There were a couple of us that became pretty close. Pete, Daniel, his girlfriend Traci, and I would hangout between classes. Pete however, was a hit or miss. He wouldn't be at class for weeks at a time. He would go from town to town and state to state following this band "Phish." They had a Grateful Dead type thing going. Whenever Pete did decide to come back he was loaded with goodies. Daniel and I bought a lot of dope from Pete and eventually acid. At first I didn't know if I could sell it or not? I had only heard stories about it and decided to buy a sheet to see how well it would sell. My friends and I got together and decided to test it out first. We took two hits apiece and for 8 hours we laughed our asses off. The next day I sold 50 hits for $10 apiece in a matter of hours. I knew then I found what I was going to build my nest egg with. Daniel had similar success. When I talked to Pete we made a deal so I could buy quantity. I bought 1000 hits for a $1,000. That's 10 sheets, and what Pete called a "Book". At $10 a hit I was making a killing. After I sold the first 100 hits the rest was profit. That was a potential profit of $9,000 for a $1,000 investment. I started putting money back to offset the extra expenses that comes with having children. I did this for a couple months before Crystal informed me of her decision to have an abortion. She told me that she was going to her mother's house in Ohio to have it done. What could I do? She was only sixteen, and I couldn't say for certain that she was making the wrong choice. I told her when she first brought it up that I would support, and stand by her in whatever decision she made, and that was what I did.

I did really well the semester after my father's death. I studied hard and completed all my assignments. I was excited to see what my final grades were going to be. I kept waiting for my grades to come in the mail. My cousin Jessie got his, Pete, Daniel, and Traci all received theirs, but I never got mine. I hadn't seen Daniel and Traci in a while. So, I thought I would drive to school, pick up my report card, and stop by their place on my way back home. I got to campus early so I would have plenty of time to do what I had to do. I didn't want to have to make another trip because I got there too late. I waited for an hour and a half before I finally got to speak to someone who could give me a straight answer. I was told the reason why I hadn't gotten my grades was because I wasn't enrolled in the fall semester. I was floored. I asked how that could be, that I had paid tuition, and my professors had me on all their attendance sheets. The school sent me a schedule of my class for Christ sakes. Of course she didn't have an answer to any of these questions. She said she would schedule me an appointment with the dean of students and he could answer any questions and address any concerns I may have. I explained to her how far I lived from the school and that "I would like to clear this matter up today" so I wouldn't have to make another trip. It didn't take me long to figure out this lady was only a parrot and incapable of making any decisions. She could only repeat over and over what she had been told to say. I knew if anyone could help me straighten this mess out it was Professor Cook. He was the professor who suggested I came to school without cleaning up first. After that we had a pretty good relationship. At least he understood the pains I had to go through to get back and forth to class.

He was coming out the door as I was coming in. I stopped him and explained to him what was going on. He told me, "follow me back to my office and we'll see if we can't get to the bottom of this." He called someone then someone else who transferred him ultimately to the Dean of Students. He told him the circumstances that lead to me not coming back to finish last semester and what a good student I have been. He told him about me working every day and driving from so far away. The Dean told Mr. Cook to send me to his office where we could set down and discuss this matter in person. When I left Mr. Cook's office I thought everything had worked itself out and the crisis had been averted. I went straight to the Dean's office where I was immediately shown into where the Dean was seated behind a very large desk. When I walked in he came from behind the desk and shook my hand, while he introduced himself, and showed me to a seat. He told me the reason why I wasn't enrolled was because I failed to go in front of some kind of student review board. I told him that this was the first time I heard of it and asked him what its purpose was. He told me it was because I failed the previous semester and it was the review board's decision that decided if I would be allowed to attend another semester at VCC. I asked, "Do you not think they would understand seeing how my father just passed away?" He immediately answered, "I'm sure they would understand such circumstances as yours." I said, "Then everything's taken care of then?" He told me it wasn't and that I was not enrolled no matter how good of a reason I had. I asked about them taking my tuition and sending me a schedule. I also asked about my name being on all the attendance sheets that my professors had. I broke my case down point by point from start to finish, but in the end it was all for naught. He told me he would allow me to enroll in the next semester, but I wouldn't receive credit for the semester I just completed. He had a very large wood desk as I hinted to before and as he said, "the decision is final." I stood up and had every intention of flipping his desk over on top of him, but when I grabbed it, it was all I could do to lift the damn thing. I managed lifting it high enough for all the contents to slide off on him and into the floor but that was it. I don't know if the secretary had called security when she overheard me raising my voice or if they just so happened to be close by, but they were on top of me in a second. The desk made a loud thud as I dropped it to the ground. As if on cue the two security guards came through the door and the Dean told them to, "escort his ass out of here and make sure he leaves school grounds. If you see him back on campus at any time call the police." They attempted to put their hands on me, but I assured them I would shoot their asses as soon as I got to my truck and to a pistol. They never touched me, but they did follow me to the parking lot where they asked me not to come back saying, "We don't want to have to call the police on you." That was the last time I ever set foot on that place.

Chapter 11

At this point things were getting pretty bad. Between the lingering memories of my father's death, the abortion, and now being told I wasn't getting credit for classes was more than I could handle. I needed a break from reality, a release, anything to take my mind off of my numerous problems. I was setting at home by myself contemplating what my next move was going to be, when I heard someone knocking at the door. I opened the door to a familiar face, it was nice to see Eric again, but it broke my heart at the same time. It was hard not to associate him with my father. He came in and started talking like old times. He asked me as he was pulling a baggie of coke out of his pocket, "Do you care if I cook this up here?" (He was referring to taking powder cocaine and turning it into crack by adding water, baking soda, and applying heat.) I had seen him and my father do this countless times in the past, and something I was very familiar with. As far as I was concerned he could do whatever he wanted, especially after refusing to sue my father's estate. That wouldn't have really mattered though. It made me feel closer to my father in some sick and twisted way. I use to set up and talk to Eric and Dad while they would cook and smoke all night. The only difference from then and now was I was setting in the seat that was once occupied by my father. I had never once dared to smoke or try it myself. Dad had told me on more than one occasion, "If I ever catch you smoking this shit I'll whip your ass" and usually there was something about him "disowning me" and my personal favorite, "do as I say not as I do" line. I very rarely disobeyed my father, because he never asked me to do or not to do something that I thought was unreasonable, and most of the time he would tell me the reasoning behind it. While Eric was still cooking, he asked, "Would it be alright if I hit this before I leave?" I told him I didn't care and after he hit it, he offered the pipe to me. I took it and hit it for the first time. We smoked a gram before he left. I didn't feel any different or any kind of effects at all. I didn't see what the big deal was or why people liked it so much. I got much higher from smoking weed and it was much cheaper.

With the abortion constantly on my mind and Dad not around to talk to, I had no one I trusted enough to talk to- much less take advice from. I was lost. Andy and his wife were constantly getting into arguments and splitting up. His driver's license had been revoked before he ever had a chance to get them. Because of this he was in constant need for someone to drive him. I was perfect for the job. He knew from my father that I kept my mouth shut and I was no idiot. He would come around early in the morning and we would start driving around making collections. If the people we were collecting from paid what they owed, he would tell them where they could go to pick up more. He would have weed hid all over the place. He hid it in paint cans that he threw out at road signs, wide spots, or at some other kind of landmark. I have known him to hide it under rocks and in the hollow of trees. He would drop off and hide packages in the middle of the night when no one expected him around. That solved two problems; one we never had more than a little to smoke on us or in the truck at any time. Two, it did no good for anyone to rat on us because we never had more than a couple thousand dollars on us. Andy wasn't concerned if they did confiscate it. A couple thousand dollars was nothing to him. Just another drop in the bucket.

Andy would also have me take him when he went to "re-up" (re-supply). I made several trips with him, but one trip in particular sticks out more than any of the rest. Andy woke me an hour or so before dawn asking if I wanted to drive him to make a pick up. I was all for it. Not only was I not doing anything that day, but road trips with Andy were fun and never boring. I was nicely compensated for these trips. He spent money freely. Not on himself as much as he did everyone else he came in contact with; especially his driver. We had to go to North Carolina which was a four hour drive from my house. That is if the traffic wasn't bad and no unforeseen or unexpected circumstances popped up. Andy told me about running in the ditch the night before and busting a tire. I asked him if we need to get another tire put on before we left because the last thing we wanted to do was be stuck on the side of the road changing a flat with forty pounds of marijuana in the bed of his truck. He said, "The tire I put on is in good shape and I threw another spare in the bed of the truck just in case we need it. We're ready to roll," or so he said.

We get to his "supplier's" house and it was a dump. Saying it was dilapidated would be an understatement. If it wasn't for the dozen cars parked in the driveway with the overflow running into the yard I would have bet money it was condemned. All of the cars were nice, except they all had thirteen inch spoked rims. Each car had at least six antennas with one or more of them well over ten feet. Andy was in the house for what I thought was an unusual amount of time. I started to get worried that something may have went wrong and was getting out of the car to make sure he was ok. When he came walking out the door. I noticed he was licking and sucking on his thumb. He got in and told me, "We're going to have to stay the night. The old man wasn't there and I don't deal with his son." I asked him what the hell he was doing sucking on his thumb like that. That's when he told me what went down.

He had found out the "old man" wasn't there and "the son", knowing Andy came to spend money, tried to persuade him into buying cocaine instead of the marijuana he came for. Andy told him that he was open to the possibility, but before he would even consider buying anything he needed a sample. He said that "the son" produced a bag of what he thought was at least three or four ounces and told Andy to "get a taste." He said, "I stuck my entire thumb in my mouth to get it wet so the coke would stick to it. I then buried it as far as it would go. The son stood there holding the bag. Staring while I dug in, wide eyed and dumb founded. I pulled it out and it had at least a gram on it. About half of which fell on the floor, before I had a chance to lick it off." When he realized what Andy had done, he started raising hell. Andy told him, "call the old man, I need to talk to him." This shut him up because he probably thought Andy was now going to make a deal on the coke. He immediately got the "old man" on the phone and Andy told him what had went down and how his son was acting because he got "a taste." Andy told him he was interested in buying some but he needed a proper sample. The "old man" assured him he would take care of it. After he spoke with his son, the son became more agreeable. Andy told me he was given a bag with what appeared to have an eight ball in it. He told "the son" that "the old man" said, "I would get a proper sample. If this is what you think is a proper sample, then I'm going to have to take my business somewhere else." This would not have been good for "the son" if Andy walked away. So "the son" got a teaspoon and proceeded to scoop spoonful after spoonful into the bag. Andy said he could see the pain on his face after he dumped each spoonful into the bag and noticed Andy was still standing there holding it open like a kid waiting to get candy on Halloween. He said he had to argue with him to get the last couple spoonful's, but what he ended up with was close to an ounce.

We left and got a motel room for the night or until he got a call saying the "old man" was back. Once we found a place, Andy called "the son" giving him the number with instructions to call him as soon as the "old man" showed up. He told him we were trying to catch rush hour traffic in the morning. The reasoning behind this is, if you're going to be transporting drugs you want to blend in and rush hour is the perfect time. It's a lot easier to blend in when you're one of hundred than it is if you're just one of ten. We got the call just after 6:00 am the next morning saying the "old man" was there. We gathered our things together leaving the room key on the table for the maid, not bothering to check out. It was early and we were in a hurry so we said, "screw it." When we pulled back into the driveway for the second time, I immediately noticed there were only two cars-not the dozen from before. Andy goes in while I stay in the car, but this time he tells me, "I may be in there for an hour or so before I'm able to get away. The "old man" likes to talk." Andy had brought enough money to buy forty pounds of marijuana. That much pot looks like a bale of hay and is impossible to hide. The best you can do is camouflage it. Needless to say I was a bit nervous. We did, however, have a pretty good plan. One Andy had used several times in the past. We had brought a hollowed out clothes dryer that was still in the box. It even had the straps on it to look like it had never been opened, but we could slip them off and put them back on with a little effort. We had been up most of the night and I had fallen asleep waiting on him. I woke up when

Andy was getting in the truck. He had something in a brown paper grocery bag and I knew it was nowhere near the amount of weed we came for. When he told me to go back to the motel that we had just left, I knew there was something up. Once we got there I went to the front desk telling them I had left the key in the room and locked myself out when I went to eat breakfast. They gave me another key. It was a damn good thing we didn't check out or there was no way we would have gotten back into that room without paying for another night. Once Andy and I were inside, he pulls out two kilos of cocaine, each about half the size of a shoebox. We start talking about where we were going to hide it, because there is a big difference between getting caught with marijuana and getting caught with cocaine. I don't care what the amount is, but two kilos was enough to put us in prison for a very long time. Andy came up with the idea of putting it inside of the spare tire we had in the back. I had heard stories of people doing it that way so, I thought it was a good idea and might work. We got the spare, two tire irons, and a big screwdriver he had in his tool box.

We let all of the air out of the tire. Using the tire irons and screwdriver, we broke one side completely away from the rim. We took both bricks, wrapped them in bed sheets, and stuffed them into opposite sides of the tire. We stuffed the tire with everything we could find to keep the bricks from shifting or moving around in case the tire was checked. We used t-shirts, blankets, sheets, and blue jeans. We stuffed it so full we liked to never got the tire back over the rim. We went to the first gas station we could find that had an air hose and pumped the tire back up.

After the drive the day before, staying up half the night and wrestling with that tire, I was worn out and falling asleep by the time we were ready to hit the road. That's when Andy pulled out the sample bag he got the day before and said, "I wasn't going to jerk this out until we got back home, but you can't hold your eyes open. I can't have you falling asleep and risk getting pulled over with all this shit on us because you nodded off." I had only snorted coke a few times in the past and then it was only in small amounts. Andy asked, "How do you want it, one big line or two little ones?" I asked if I could have two medium sized ones, and he began to laugh while he poured out two lines that consisted of more coke than all I had ever done in the past combined. Obviously my idea of what constituted a big or small line was different from his. After I got these lines down, sleep wasn't an option, and about ever twenty minutes he would cut out two more for me, and two for himself. After about an hour, every car that got behind me looked like a cop. We did this all the way home.

We came through the last little town and thought we were home free, when the unexpected happened. We got a flat! I pulled off the side of the road and even though we were in familiar territory, it didn't take away from the fact that we were setting on the side of the road with a flat and our spare was stuffed full of clothes and cocaine. We were less than five miles from my house so Andy said, "Fuck it, that shit is packed in there really well, and there are so many clothes in between each of them, there is no way they are going to shift. Let's try it! We will just have to take it easy. It's going to be rough because the tire is so out of balance, but I think we can make it to your house." We changed the tire and he was right about it being rough. If I went over 20 mph the truck shook so bad I couldn't keep it on the road. It took twenty minutes to get to my house, but we made it. We took the tire off and broke it down in my kitchen. We were expecting the coke to be busted all to hell, but to our surprise it was all intact and not damaged in the least.

Andy and I had decided to go to his Brother Donnie's house to do the rest of the "sample" which was about a half of an ounce. Before we left he wanted to cut out a few ounces. He knew of some people close by that would buy some: so we cut half of one of the bricks down into ounces. We went to breaking it down and after ten minutes we both started feeling the effects of handling all that uncut cocaine with our bare hands. I first started tasting it, and then my mouth went numb. Before I knew it I was getting short of breath and my heart was racing. We had to wash our hands to slow down the effects before we overdosed. It was so bad we had to buy rubber gloves before we could finish.

We went to Donnie's and cut out a few lines before Donnie suggested that we cook "some" up and smoke it. Andy didn't give a shit and it made no difference to me one way or the other. I had only smoked it once before with Eric and didn't get much out of it. If it was up to me I would have just snorted it, but it wasn't, and I thought I might have done it wrong the first time. Donnie and Andy both hit it and commented on how good it was. So, when Donnie handed me the pipe, I put a piece on it about as big as the end of my finger and slowly started to inhale as much as I could before I ran out of breath. I held it as long as I could before I exhaled, and apparently I did do something wrong before, because it was much different this time. As I exhaled, I started becoming light headed, my mouth began to water and even though everything sounded like I was in a tunnel I heard a distant ringing. I later found out that was what was referred to as getting "a ringer." Andy stayed around for a couple hours before he had to leave and "take care of business." He did leave the rest of the "sample" there for Donnie and me. We stayed up all night-talking and smoking.

Chapter 12

When Andy came by he would generally stay for a week, sometimes two before he would make his way back home. It may be a couple of days, up to a month, before I would see him again. It was all according to when and how bad of a fight he and his wife had that prompted him to leave. It went like this. If it was a long, drawn out, bad intentional fight then the cool down period between reconciliation would be longer, and vice-versa for the little spats.

In between these times I would hang out with Donnie. He basically came to my house attempting to keep the interaction and contact between the people who were associated with drugs and drug use away from his wife and child. More often than not Andy, Donnie, and I would end up together; getting high of course.

The major difference between Andy and Donnie, is Donnie is not a sociable person, to say the very least. While Dad was still alive, Donnie would stop by and if someone was there he didn't know or only knew in passing, he would walk straight out the back door without ever saying a word. Dad would immediately get rid of whoever was there and we would go find Donnie. He would normally be standing on a little walk bridge my father and I had built so we could get across the creek to our dogs. It was also common to see him petting and playing with one or more of them. If one of them had knocked over their water dishes or a bowl was empty, he would be down in the creek refilling their bowls. Donnie was a dog lover and like my father and I, he especially liked bulldogs.

Like I had said earlier, if I wasn't with Donnie I was with Andy. We would be out riding around, hustling, and smoking. We would be out collecting or dropping off, and usually it was both, but we were also having a good time. Everyone liked seeing Andy come around. Whenever we would stop to take care of business, he would smoke and give away hundreds of dollars of coke. If he would see a child running around he would more often than not call them over and give them ten or twenty dollars just to see their little faces light up. I don't see how he ever made any money. He once told me when he and I would go out collecting he would go through around three ounces a day. It would take Andy and me days to finish making "the rounds." If he and his wife were fighting and they usually were, it was more likely than not for me to drop him off at some woman's house that we met during the past day or so. He would tell me a certain day and time to be back to pick him up. Usually all he said was, "I'll get up with you in a day or two. Take my truck and drive it like it's yours." Before I would go home to get some much needed sleep he would give me a couple 8 balls and at least a hundred dollars. If he didn't show up when he said he would, I would go looking for him. It wasn't uncommon for the people he was with to act like they couldn't give him a ride. They knew when he left, the party was over, and he knew it was only a matter of time before I found him, and most of the time he would be right where I left him.

By this time, Donnie was selling a little coke as well. His wife, who was straight as an arrow, was dead set against it. Donnie only dealt with a few people, but he had a small child, and didn't need him to be around that sort of thing. I never saw her take so much as a sip of beer, come to think of it; I never heard her even curse. I don't think she really cared if Donnie got high; it was the people that came with it she couldn't stand. She was never rude to anyone and was very kind to me. She always asked if I would like something to drink, and if she was cooking, offer me a plate.

To keep the peace and the undesirable element away from her and his son, Donnie, I, and a few others built a shed at the end of his property. It was well built despite all the materials being salvaged and reused. He put a picnic table under it, hung a few flower pots here and there, and even ran electricity to it. We had a light and a receptacle that we used to play the radio. Eventually someone gave him some bamboo type blinds so at night he could roll them down and it would block almost all of the light and was hardly noticeable from the road. It was summer and would have looked really suspicious if there was a bunch of us crowded around an out building. So, that's why he elected to build a shed and decorate it like he did. After he put on all the finishing touches it looked like one of the sheds you see at the park or at anyone's house. It was up on a little hill, beside a wide spot in the road. Donnie chose the perfect location. You could see who was coming up the hill or what the people were doing in the wide spot, but they couldn't see you. I can remember staying in that shed for days at a time. It seemed like every time I went home after partying for two or three days, as soon as I went to sleep Andy would be there to wake me up and start the partying all over.

I know this may sound crazy, but if it wasn't for them keeping me busy and my mind off my problems, there is no telling what I may have done. Even though keeping busy and my mind occupied consisted of selling dope and getting high, it still beat the alternative of eating a bullet. I know Andy and Donnie both ended up liking and trusting me, but in the beginning it was because of the friendship and loyalty they shared with my father that they took an interest in me and my well-being.

Andy was constantly on the move. He was always on his way somewhere and you can bet he would be hustling every step of the way. I never met anyone who could keep up with him. I was fifteen years younger than him and I couldn't hold a light to him, but I put forth a hell of an effort. One time I stayed up with him eight days and nights before I had to tap out. During those eight days the only thing either of us ate was a cheeseburger and we split that. It took two days of telling him I needed to take a break before I finally talked him into dropping me off at my mother's house.

For the first time in over a week I was able to eat a decent meal. Cocaine suppresses the appetite to where you not only can't eat, but it changes the taste of food to where you don't want to. After I ate as much as I could, I took a shower and lay down in my old bed to finally get some sleep. As soon as my head hit the pillow I immediately fell into a deep comfortable sleep. It seemed like I had just closed my eyes when I was woken by Andy saying, "wake up and hit this, you've slept long enough." I was wiping the sleep out of my eyes as he handed me a pipe. I took a big hit and was instantly awake. I got dressed and spent four more days with him. By the fourth day, my body was spent. I had reached my limit. In twelve days I slept maybe five hours and could physically take no more. I slept for two days.

It was a couple of weeks before I saw Andy again. When I finally did see him he looked like hell. He had lost at least twenty pounds and told me he was recovering from staying up for twenty- seven straight days. By looking at him I believed every word. His cheeks and eyes were sunken in and his clothes looked two sizes too big. I can attest for twelve days of the twenty seven and he had been at it for a week before that.

Andy and his wife were on and off, but he really did love her so he tried every way he could to make it work. Despite all of his efforts, it was a constant struggle and he even suspected she was stealing from him. I tried to keep my involvement in his relationship to a bare minimum. Every once in a while he would ask for my advice about one thing or another, but for the most part he kept his problems to himself.

Donnie and I were at his house partying when he received a call from Andy about 5:00 in the morning. He asked if Donnie and I would come and pick him up. His truck had a flat, he and his wife were fighting and he needed to, "get the fuck away from this crazy bitch," as he so eloquently put it. When we got there they had made up a little and Andy was telling her that he had to go make "the rounds" so he could re-up. She wasn't going to let him out of her sight; so we all left to go back to Donnie's. Andy and his wife were in her car and Donnie and me in my truck. When we got back to Donnie's, Andy and his wife were fighting like mortal enemies. We had planned for Andy to go to my house, and then Donnie and I would come and meet him. Before Andy left he took the distributor cap and wires off his wife's car. That way she couldn't follow him. He figured she would call someone for a ride back to their house. When he was finished taking care of business, he could replace the cap and wires and go on home.

We were at my house making plans and getting high for at least an hour before Andy asked if I would drive by Donnie's to see if his wife was still there. When I pulled in the driveway I could see her outside looking under the hood of her car. When she saw me she came over asking if I knew where Andy was. I told her, "That's who I'm looking for." I told her that he was probably at Joey's, that I overheard him say he had to stop off there first. We spoke for a few minutes before she asked if I would be interested in making five pounds of pot. I told her, "I would be very interested." She told me she had stolen ten ounces of coke and five pounds of pot from Andy and if I would take her to get it she would give me the marijuana. I told her I would, but I had to make sure Andy was nowhere around. I told her, "Andy will shoot me if he caught me with you." Before I left she handed me fifty dollars to pick up a bag of coke before I came back to get her. I went back to my house and told Andy what she has asked me to do and gave him the fifty dollars. What we needed to know was where she had the stuff hid. He gave me some coke and I went back to smoke it with her and to see if I could find out where we were going. I told her Andy was at Joey's, but he was getting ready to leave. She told me the general area of where we were going and suggested we take the back way through the mountains to avoid being seen. After we smoked what she had bought, I told her I was going to go make sure Andy was gone before she got in the car with me. I went to tell Andy what I learned and which way she suggested we go. Andy and Donnie went ahead and stopped about half-way across the mountain to wait for us. When we met Andy was going to get in with us and make her tell where she had the stuff hid.

The way she suggested we go was perfect. It was very out of the way and once you passed the last house, there were no more houses for several miles. It was a short cut across the mountain that Andy and I used very often. Everything went as planned. We were in the middle of nowhere when we met Donnie and Andy. She kept telling me to say I was just taking her home. She kept repeating "tell him you're taking me home" over and over as we pulled up next to one another. She knew she was fucked when Andy got out of the car and came around to the passenger side of my truck. As he got in I got out, but not before taking the keys with me. Andy slapped her a few times, but it was only after she lied right to his face. She tried to get me to go along with the story about taking her home, but I quickly told her she was lying and she had been set up. I told her the best thing she could do is be honest and give Andy the stuff back. Even though Andy did slap her a few times, it was nowhere near the beating I thought she was going to get. He told Donnie he was going to get in with me and that, "I'm going to kill this bitch if she doesn't tell me where my shit is." The way Donnie looked at me when Andy told him this made me believe that was his intentions. I had already gone too far to turn back now. At this point I was either with him or against him and I wasn't against him!

We drove deeper into the mountains and were passing the pipe back and forth the whole time. Occasionally he would tell his wife that if she would, "shut that fucking whining up," he would give her a "puff" as he called it. She would stop long enough to take a hit, but start crying again as soon as Andy started telling her what he was going to do to her if she didn't come clean. She kept telling him that she had never taken anything that she was lying to me to get me to take her home. All of the sudden Andy told me, "stop the fucking truck, I'm going to blow this bitch's brains out if she so much as thinks about telling me another lie." Before I had a chance to stop, she jumped over Andy and out the door, running for what I'm sure what she thought was her life. Andy caught her and had her pinned down and told me,

"Bring me something to tie this bitch up with." I looked all over the inside and of my truck trying to find him something. I couldn't find a piece of rope or tape, but I did have a spot light I used to poach deer. I had just added twenty extra foot of cord to it a few days before, so I cut it off and was taking it to him, when out of nowhere this old couple came driving by. Andy had his wife downed in the ditch line and here I was dragging twenty foot of cord behind me on my way to where they were. They stopped and asked if everything was ok, and as soon as they did, Andy's old lady started yelling, "He's going to kill me," and "call the police; help!" I explained to them that he had caught her cheating on him, that she was only being dramatic. Needless to say we couldn't tie her up now. We had been seen and no telling if they were going to call the cops as soon as they got to a phone or not. We all got back in the truck and she swore to him that there was no dope. I guess he believed her, because he told me to turn around and go back the way we came. When we got back out on the main road and stopped at the intersection, he put her out telling her she could find her own way home.

A few months later Andy and his girlfriend were on their way to re-up. His soon to be ex-wife found out where he was going and what he had planned, so she called the police on him. The police stopped him and searched his truck. They didn't find any drugs, but they did find thirty thousand dollars in cash. His girlfriend had a little bit of baking soda in a bag in her purse. Because of the baking soda being in a bag, they claimed he was selling fake cocaine and basically one was as bad as the other. Even though the baking soda was found on his girlfriend, they offered Andy a deal where he could take the blame and get six months in the county jail. Until he could prove where the thirty thousand dollars came from, it was considered drug money and, therefore, confiscated.

When Andy got out of jail all his fair-weather friends turned their backs on him now that he had nothing to give them. I offered to let him stay at my house which he did for a while until he got back with his ex-wife. When he got out of jail he seemed changed in some way. It was nothing I could describe or put my finger on. He was just different. His ex-wife ended up dying that Christmas. They were having Christmas dinner with her family when she choked on a piece of ham. Andy was there and did everything he could do to save her, but it wasn't meant to be.

Donnie lived close by and I visited him regularly. He was always working on some kind of car and still not very sociable. As a matter of fact, we rode to work together every day. He was the one who got me the job working in the coal mines when all of this mess went down.

Chapter 13

A few years before my father died he was involved in an automobile accident that left him in severe and constant pain. The lady that hit him was returning home after having cataract surgery. With her vision impaired, she should never have been behind the wheel. The last years of my father's life was riddled with pain. We weren't taking our 'Sunday drives" anymore and if I went fishing, I had to go alone. I would sometimes go to keep from wasting the bait. Every time I went without Dad it felt like I was cheating on him. It was almost the same kind of guilt you would feel after cheating on your wife or girlfriend. I made myself a promise long ago not to ever cheat. So, I haven't really been fishing since my father died. I know it's not the same thing but it feels like it is and that's close enough for me.

I couldn't tell you how many times I have awakened in the early morning hours to moans and other sounds of pain as my father crawled on his hands and knees to the bathroom. I tried to help, but there was no help for him. He couldn't stand to be straightened up or be on his feet for any length of time; if at all!

Dad sued the lady's insurance and there may have been someone else but I'm not really for sure. What I am sure of is that they settled out of court and dad's cut was one hundred-fifty thousand dollars. Since my father had passed away and I was his closest living relative and only son, the money and everything else he owned came to me. I didn't get it all at once. It took about six months. I was spending the money almost as quickly as I got it. Having it spaced out helped me realize the money wasn't going to last forever and by the time I got the last payment I had wised up a little. The first check was for seventy-five thousand dollars and I went through it in about four months. I bought motorcycles, boats, four-wheelers, and anything else I could think of or want. I spent some money on furniture and paint, but that was about it for the house. It never occurred to me to buy a car until a few months went by and the weather turned cold. I was riding my bike everywhere I went. I had a beautiful black GSXR 1100 and it would outrun the word of God. Every time I got on it I felt like I was on a roller coaster. I could do 100 mph in second gear and it had six of them. It wasn't long before I had accumulated three reckless driving tickets. Two of them were for riding wheelies in town and the other which was more serious was for going 128 mph in a 45 mph zone. I spoke to all of the officers involved and they all agreed to drop the charges if I would get rid of my bike. So I was forced to sell it. When I say forced, I mean if I didn't sell it and get the reckless driving charges dropped I would have lost my license and couldn't legally ride it anyway.

The truck I had served a purpose of getting me from one place to the other, but it was starting to look rough and it was only a matter of time before it started breaking down. The weekend I sold my bike I took twenty five thousand dollars and my friend Dustin to buy a car. I really wanted one of the new Ram Air TransAms and had every intention of getting one. Dustin's father took him and I car shopping that weekend and everywhere we stopped they wouldn't let me test drive the cars I wanted to buy. After we were turned down the first couple of times, I started showing them the stack of money as I was walking out of the door. A few of them chased after me once they saw all that money. Car salesmen work on commission and it broke their hearts to see cold hard cash walk out the door. We stopped at least half dozen places with the same result every time I asked for a test drive. Finally after searching all day I found what I was looking for.

As we pulled into the parking lot of the last dealership I noticed on the show room floor at the adjacent car lot a red Trans Am. The only thing was it was a used car lot and I wanted something new. I looked around the dealership where we were and didn't see anything I liked. I decided to go check out the car I saw at the used car place and as soon as I walked into the showroom I knew I was going to buy it. A salesman came out and I explained to him that I have been looking all day for the right car and thought that maybe I had found it, but I needed to take it for a test drive before I could be certain. He said, "Let me go get the keys," and off he went without any smartass comments or answers. He came back, handed me the keys, and proceeded to open the big glass doors that were for the most part the front of the showroom. While he was doing this he went on to tell me the owner of the car was also the owner of the dealership across the street. The car was practically brand new. It only had 1100 miles on it and the guy only drove it to and from work as a promotional type of thing. Despite the car being two years old it still had that new car smell. Dustin and I got in, and as we were pulling out the salesman stopped us saying, "I have to ride with you." I didn't care if he came or not at this point, I was happy to finally be test driving a car. Dustin opened the passenger door and leaned forward holding the seat giving the salesman a little room and assistance getting in. The salesman stood there looking bewildered and Dustin asked, "What are you waiting for, climb in." He told Dustin that he wasn't allowed to ride in the back that it was the dealerships policy that he ride in the front passenger seat. Dustin got in the back just to hurry the process along. He didn't like it at all. For a second I thought Dustin was going to sucker punch him by the way he was looking at him. As soon as we hit the first red light, it was on. I pealed out and left two black marks for over a hundred feet and two more about the length of the car when I hit second. I knew then I had to have it. At that moment I fell in love. When I pulled in the salesman was telling me to pull in the front and was pointing at parking spaces as I drove by them. The salesman asked where I was going and I told him, "I need to check something out." Once around back at the garage area where there were only few cars and lots of space. I geared down, whipped the steering wheel, and floored it. I did one donut one way and another the other, all the while the salesman and Dustin were both screaming. Dustin for joy and the salesman for his life! He was screaming, trying to grab the shifter (which is why I changed directions of the donuts) and begging me to stop all at the same time. When I stopped he told me to, "Get the fuck out of the car." He said this two or three times before I told him to, "shut the fuck up, I'm going to take it." Dustin was in the back laughing his ass off and when he heard me say that he reach over the front seat, pecked the sales guy on the shoulder and tells him, "Now you can get the fuck out of my seat, badass!" It was the funniest thing I ever heard. So much so, the salesman himself started laughing.

Chapter 14

It took me all of about three months to wreck the Transam, but I replaced it with a beautiful corvette. By the time I bought the corvette I had blown practically all of the money I had gotten. I had received it all except for about thirty thousand dollars. I was expecting to get it in the next few months.

It was about this time that my cousin, Shea, moved back to West Virginia. He had lived in North Carolina for the last three or four years where he worked for a building construction company. He did very well there and worked his way up the ladder to the point that he had his own crew. Somehow he fell off a lift or scaffold and injured his ankle, knee, and hip. He went months without it getting any better. In fact it was getting worse. His movement was more limited and the pain more severe. He went to several doctors and they could not figure out what was hindering his recovery. He took every test and x-ray under the sun, before they found the tumor. They told him he had a year to live!

The compensation he was getting for the injury to his leg ended, because it was the cancer that was preventing him from getting better, not the actual injury itself. No more checks or medical care of any kind. He and his wife fought with them for months with no success. With only a year to live, he gave up fighting with Worker's Compensation and moved back to West Virginia.

Shea's wife was very loving and loyal, even though she was about half crazy. She cared for him in a way I think only she could. Shea didn't like having people around him: the only person he was comfortable around was his wife. Shea was too proud to ever ask for help, but I didn't give him a chance or option. I did what I saw needed to be done before he could tell me any differently. I had some money put back and was hustling a little here and there to pick up some extra cash when I could. Since I wasn't working, I started going down to Shea's more and more to see if I could do anything for him. At first it was maybe to mow the grass, which only took fifteen minutes at the most, or to change the oil in his car. For the most part, it was little jobs that his wife would have done if given a chance. Most of the time we would just set around, watch movies, talk, and smoke weed. His doctor actually encouraged his marijuana use because it helped with his appetite.

The tumor had a major effect on his senses; especially his sense of taste and smell. There were certain smells that he couldn't stand and cigarette smoke was one of them. As the tumor grew, so did the sensitivities. At first I took off my jacket or sweater and left it on the porch, but it wasn't long before I had to take my T-shirt off as well. I would leave three or four T-shirts at his house just to have something to put on that he could withstand.

He would also have cravings for strawberry shortcake sundaes. I drove by the place that made them on the way to his house; the only problem was there was a thirty minute drive that separated them. In between his sundae cravings he would drink cans of Ensure even though he didn't particularly care for it, but he knew he had to take in some kind of nourishment. We would open a can and put a straw in it. He would take only one sip. His wife and I would beg and plead with him saying, "please just one more sip; for me." That usually worked and he would drink all he could stomach: but if we tried it again he would call us on it saying, "Do you think I'm stupid, don't try that shit again." Or when he saw one of us go to pick the can up it would be, "I told you I don't want any more of that shit, so put it down."

No one could get a sundae to Shea's house before it melted, except for me. What took everyone else thirty minutes I could do in fifteen, sometimes even ten minutes, if there was no traffic. I put that corvette to good use; it hugged those country roads. Plus I put it in a little cooler I bought just for the purpose of transporting sundaes. I had gel ice packs to keep from crushing and getting water into the container that held his sundae. I would only get a call once or twice a week and half the time once I got it there he couldn't stand to eat it.

It broke my heart to see Shea deteriorating right before my eyes and knowing there was nothing I could do for him. I never saw anyone go through something so evil. He was in constant pain. His life was being taken slowly and deliberately. He knew he was dying and saying he embraced it, would be the wrong word to use I think, but he knew death was inevitable. He accepted it with the heart of a warrior that only few could understand. It's hard for me to imagine anyone having more dignity or courage. Watching him go through what he did with his head held high and not giving an inch, that is what taught me it wasn't always how a man lives that defines him; it was also how he dies. He never broke down, cursed God, or asked, "Why me?" I pray when my time comes, I, too, can face death with such bravery.

As the tumor grew he became more impaired and lost the feeling and use of one side of his body. With the use of only one arm and not being able to walk very well, he couldn't do a lot. Like my father, Shea loved to fish. He lived beside the river so I tried to take him whenever he felt like going. He had an electric wheelchair that he would ride down to where we had to cross the railroad track. When we got there I would carry his wheelchair across and help him to the other side. I use to screw with him and pile all the fishing gear on his lap. He would tell me, "This is a wheelchair, not a pickup truck." Every time we went, the river was about half ass muddy and we never caught anything. Basically we were drowning worms. He and I both enjoyed our "fishing trips." He would say, "If nothing else, I like sitting by the river and talking," and I loved to listen.

With his mobility getting more limited by the day, he was able to do less and less. I was constantly trying to come up with things that would entertain him. One bright idea was to buy him a dart board. I set it up in his living room. After a few games we were able to establish where he needed to sit in order to compensate for his limited mobility. At first he was a little apprehensive, but once we started playing and he saw that I wasn't going to just let him win to make him feel good, he got into it. He was competitive as hell. When I was there and he felt up to it, we were more than likely playing darts. When I would call to check on him, Shelia would tell me that Shea had been practicing. He started calling me more and more asking if I wanted to come down and hangout. I knew hanging out consisted of him beating me in darts, because after a couple weeks I couldn't beat him. When he was feeling bad, I would tell him I wanted to play him then, not when he was feeling good. He would tell me, "You should be ashamed of yourself for trying to take advantage of a sick man," or that, "You need to use this time to practice."

His health deteriorated to the point of where he needed around the clock care. So, I moved in more or less. He had a big house with several spare bedrooms. I would stay up nights. About eight or nine o'clock his wife would wake up and fix breakfast, of which Shea could almost never get down. By the time breakfast was ready and all of the smells started mingling together, it would kill his appetite- if it didn't make him sick. Hospice started giving him this thick liquid they called NTV which stood for Nutrition Through Veins. They installed a permanent IV and put him on a morphine pump. They showed his wife and me how to administer it: twice a day we would inject a 10 cc syringe of NTV into his IV. His wife's sister was a nurse, so arrangements were made with hospice for her to oversee the medical things his wife and I couldn't.

Shea's wife and I got along very well. I cannot remember having so much as a disagreement with her. Basically I did whatever she asked of me. She was as Shea called her his "Angel". Her whole world revolved around Shea. She thought about him and his wellbeing in everything she did.

Just before his death he was so weak and frail from not eating he didn't have the strength to put a dip of snuff in his mouth. As I said earlier, Shea never asked for help and I was a little taken back when he asked me if I would put a dip of snuff in his mouth. It got to me that he was so weak and I started to choke up a little, but because as Shea so delicately put it, "I can't stand all that fucking crying." I got a hold of myself before my emotions got the better of me. I put the dip in his mouth. His now deep set dark eyes looked at me in a different way than I ever saw him look at anyone before. I held a cup to his mouth so he could spit and as he did his gaze never left mine and out of nowhere said, "You're my hero." It was at that moment that I understood. He was dying. I knew it was inevitable, but I never accepted it. I couldn't hold it any longer. I broke down and began to cry, telling him how much I love him. He never told me to "stop that damn crying" as I heard him tell everyone else. He let me go because I believe he knew it couldn't be helped, it spewed out of me uncontrollably, but after a few minutes I regained my composure. It was the way he looked at me more than what he said that touched me. In his own way he was thanking me and saying goodbye. That one moment paid for everything I ever did for him a thousand times over. It was by far the most humbling and touching moment of my life.

For the last four months of Shea's life, he, his wife, and I were extremely close. They told people, "We wouldn't trade Charlie for anything." I had started preparing myself for Shea's death the best I knew how. It took a lot out of me as well as the rest of the family; especially his mother. When she would come to see him, she would break down crying. She is a sweet, God-fearing woman that could not control her emotions around him. She would start crying for no reason. Shea told her, "If you're going to cry every time you come down her I wish you wouldn't come." I can only guess to his reasoning behind telling her that was because the only thing that could break his resolve was seeing his mother cry. To him being "strong" was the key to everyone else being "strong." If he lost control then everyone else would as well, and, to the end he was a rock.

My one regret was that I was not there the hour of his death. I had made plans for a month to go to Tennessee to pick up some coke. I wasn't working and I needed to make a quick flip so I could get my money right before I went broke. When I left to go to Tennessee, I told Shea I would be back the following night, but once I got down there things got delayed and I had to stay an extra day to get what I went for. He was doing better than I seen him do in a long time. When I got back in town, I stopped off at Shea's mother's house to see how he was doing and that's when I found out he passed away a few hours before I made it back.

Chapter 15

After he graduated from high school my cousin, Chris, came to live with me. Shea's brother, Kenneth, was away at college, but he came home at least two weekends a month. Then there was Dustin. He was something else. He was constantly trying to make his friends laugh and smile, but he was no "laughing boy." His girlfriend and I lived a few miles apart, so he had to pass my house whether he was coming from or going to see her. Her dad didn't allow her to have Dustin come over during the week. Her mother was more lenient, as long as Dustin was gone before her dad got home from work. He didn't get home until midnight so it wasn't like he was missing any time with her. He went to see her every night: every night on his way back home he would stop by the house. I could set my watch by what time he arrived. Chris and I used to make bets on how long it was going to take for him to start singing and dancing when he came in. Once he got that out of his system, we would start making plans for the rest of the night; which usually consisted of us going somewhere to spot-light deer. We knew spot-lighting was illegal, but we looked at it as performing a community service.

When we went it was because we knew someone who either needed or wanted the meat. Kinda like Robinhood would have been doing if he had a spotlight and automatic rifle. To offset the cost of gas, ammunition, and beer we would sell some of the deer meat to the local bars. For fifty dollars we would give them two front shoulders, two back hams, and the back straps. They never wanted the neck or ribs. The local hunters were sensitive about killing their deer especially their big bucks. A few of them would ask us not to go here or there because that is where they were hunting. The hunters around the house would put in serious time scouting, tracking, and hunting specific deer. So, we would respect their requests and made it a point to never shoot anything with horns.

Dustin, Chris, and I were out one night riding around killing time. I had a pistol on me, so we decided to ride over to the lake and see if we could spot a deer close enough to shoot with a handgun. The only thing we couldn't decide on was who was going to get the first shot. To settle this dilemma we began playing a heated game of rock-paper-scissors. We were caught up in the game when, wham, a deer jumps out in front of us. Because Dustin was concentrating more on the game we were playing than on the road, we hit the deer going 40 mph. He came to a screeching halt and was cursing like a sailor. Dustin pulled over and he and I got out examining the car while Chris went to check out the deer. The bumper of the car was pushed in and the parking light was broken, but all in all it wasn't in too bad a shape. Dustin loved this car and he sunk every penny he made in it. It was one of those old school Oldsmobiles. Whenever he would get a speck of dirt on it, he would try to wash the paint off of it! Even though his car wasn't hurt that bad, Dustin was heartbroken.

Chris came to see what the damage was and reported that the deer was dead. Dustin had an old garbage bag in the trunk and he suggested we tear it down the side and bottom to make it big enough to line the trunk of his car. Then we could lay the deer on it. The deer wasn't bleeding anywhere except a little out of its mouth, so he didn't have to worry about getting blood everywhere. I asked Dustin, "Are you sure you want to put a deer in the trunk of your car?" He responded with, "Hell yea, I'm going to eat that son of a bitch, you seen what it did to my car." Chris and I started laughing, but Dustin was dead serious.

We got the deer into the trunk. We started back to my house with the intentions of cutting the deer up and having fresh venison. It took Dustin a minute for him to find the humor in his comment about eating the S.O.B. We were joking and laughing about the whole situation trying mostly to ease Dustin's pain about his car. Then all of the sudden we hear a thud. At first I thought it was a flat tire, but after a few more beats and bangs that thought was quickly discarded. The noises didn't have any sort of rhythm or consistency like a flat tire would. It took me a second to realize the noise was coming from the trunk. That damn deer was only knocked out, not dead like Chris had said. When we stopped and got out, we all gathered around the trunk of the car, listening to these noises in bewilderment. I suggested, after I got my senses back, that we open the trunk, and try to shoot it when it jumps out. We were throwing ideas back and forth as the noises were getting louder and louder. The deer must have gotten on its back somehow, because the sound of the noises started changing. Now with every loud thud we saw a dent pop up on the trunk lid. Dustin was hysterical after the first dent, but he was practically losing his mind after the second, third, and forth one popped up. He quickly ran to the glove box, grabbed my pistol and as he was coming back around the car, tossed Chris the keys, yelling to him, "Pop the trunk and get out of the way." He chambered a round as Chris put the key into the lock. They looked at one another for a second before Dustin said, "Pop it." As soon as he saw fur, he commenced to shooting. Before the trunk was completely open Dustin had emptied a fifteen shot clip into the trunk of his car. Then he walked over and slammed the trunk shut. I couldn't believe what I just saw. As Chris and I stood there dumbfounded, we came back to ourselves with the smell of gasoline. That's when we saw a pool of gas mixed with blood forming under the car.

Dustin had not only killed the deer, but he also managed to put a dozen holes straight through the floor board and at least four of them pierced the gas tank. With the gas pouring out from under the car, we made it within a few miles of Dustin's house. We were on the outskirts of town; in a few hours people were going to be going to work. We had to do something. We were about three miles from my house. So, we decided Chris and I should walk and get my truck then come back and tow Dustin home.

When we got out of the car, we noticed that we had left a four foot wide gas and blood trail that was visible even in the dark. It looked like something from a Quentin Tarantino movie. As soon as we returned and hooked his car to my truck, the police pulled in to see what the problem was. When the cop saw all of the blood and before we could explain what had happened, he pulled his gun on us and called for backup. When his back up arrived they handcuffed us and put us in the back of their cars. Chris and I were in one and Dustin in the other. They questioned us and I guess our story matched Dustin's. I didn't see how we could have gotten in too much trouble from telling them the truth, because there was no denying what happened. When they finally opened the trunk and saw we had been telling them the truth all along, they didn't take us to jail or even write a ticket. They let us go saying they felt sorry for us and thought we had suffered enough. That's not to say they didn't laugh their asses off every time they saw me.

A few months later Dustin was killed in a car accident. It was only by chance that I wasn't with him. We would go over in this big bottom by the river and do donuts at least once a week. He had another little front wheel drive car that he would play around in. You can only do donuts in a front wheel drive car two ways. One is by doing them in reverse. The other is by getting your speed up driving forwards and whip the wheel at the same time pulling the emergency brake. We liked to do a combination of the two. We liked to get up to 35-40 mph and pull the emergency brake. Once we would start to go around in circles, we would shift the car into reverse and floor it. We had done this countless times in the past, and never had any problems, much less an accident.

The night of his death the car caught hold instead of spinning around. Dustin had his window down and didn't have his seatbelt on. When the car flipped, his head got caught between the top of the car and the ground. Dustin was my closest friend and the third person I had lost in the past year. He was twenty-one.

Chapter 16

By now I had been working in the mines for a while. One night I had a big piece of rock fall and injure my back. I was constantly in pain and taking pain medication. Some of the pain was due to old sports injuries: like 2 broken legs and two knee surgeries. So I was familiar with pain medication. Due to self-medication, I was familiar with just about any type of meds. I was prescribed a new pain medication called oxycontin (Hillbilly Heroin). For pain management it was extremely effective and long lasting. It wasn't long before the demand grew to an overwhelming state inside the illegal drug community.

About this time an old friend from high school, Casey, came back to West Virginia. Right after graduation, he joined the Marines. A couple years in, he injured his hand and thumb in some sort of training exercise. After this he didn't have proper use of his thumb and was medically discharged. He came back home to his family, girlfriend, and two children.

We had only heard of heroin down in southern West Virginia by word of mouth and through movies. I had never seen it in any kind of quantity. As for Casey and I we were ignorant of the effects of long term opioid use. Neither of us was told by anyone that we would build up a tolerance and dependence for oxycontin. We thought it was like smoking marijuana. If you didn't have it, you just didn't have it: no side effects or physical dependence. I knew about antibiotics, anti-inflammatory, and sinus medication, and you didn't get physically ill if you didn't have any of those.

It wasn't until I ran out that the harsh reality slapped me in the face. The "Oxy" fad was now a full blown epidemic.

After I found out how "sick" and bad I felt if I ran out, my hustle went to a whole new level. Casey and I found out we were birds of a feather. We began hustling together; at first he knew people I didn't, and vice-versa. One of my father's friends told me years later, "If I had the same drive to succeed as I did to find a pill, I would have been a millionaire long ago." The people who couldn't afford their habit began to rob and steal. I have seen otherwise good people turn into liars and thieves. I have seen beautiful, respectable girls turn into whores overnight.

That's not to mention the informants. In our little corner of the world the police were and still are as crooked as the thieves, robbers, and drug addicts. What they were taking was not material possessions, but people's freedom of choice and their dignity. I'm not saying there aren't good cops out there, but only that it's been my experience that they are few and far between. I have been told by girls I went to high school with and some that were still in high school, about cops pulling them over for no reason or for some kind of made up bullshit. They would scare them by threatening to write them a ticket and most of the time that served their purpose. If they got them worked up enough about a ticket, they wouldn't have to mention anything about "taking them in" or jail. The ones who were not so easily scared, they would handcuff, and put in the back of the police cruisers, while they searched their cars. The excuse was "searching for drugs." Whether they found anything or not they would say they did. All of the girls I talked to who would admit, or even talk about it, said they would give them the line of, "maybe we can work something out." We would try to make light of the situation by joking about that line being in the police handbook under standard operational procedure for cops who couldn't get laid. What they were doing and I'm sure still are, is raping young girls, some of whom were still in high school. That's not to mention all of the stories I heard from the women who were drug addicts. They use to tell me of cops trading pills they confiscated for sex. They would even go seeking these cops out, wanting to make another trade. None of the girls I talked to would ever file charges on them because they would have to go to the police station to do it and they said they were afraid of what they would do to them. They were the cops after all, and even more vindictive than a woman. That goes to show you the quality of cop we had running around. They preyed on young helpless girls and drug addicts. The cops I knew were worse than thieves, at least with a thief you know what you're getting. I was under the belief that cops were supposed to be held to a higher standard. They were nothing more than low life bullies and rapists with a badge. They would talk and say nasty shit about these high school girls they screwed when no one could hear them, trying to piss me off. Especially at football games, where I had the most contact with them: unintentional contact, and unwanted contact, by the way. Needless to say, I had absolutely no respect for any law enforcement. I don't condone what and how they trapped these girls. I knew right from wrong and could handle any problem that came my way so I had no use for them.

Casey and I saw things very similarly about most all things. Dad told me when I was very young and had repeated it to me on a regular basis that, "an argument is the first step to a fight, do not argue, knock his fucking brains out." I simply did not argue, I fought-period. I didn't argue with women so why would I with a man. Casey or I didn't tolerate being talked rough to or screamed at.

As you can probably tell my father had a reputation as a fighting man. A reputation is a funny thing. Once he had it, the more people wanted to try him out. An itch that only took a second to be scratched. Casey and I went to the bar one night while my dad was still alive, and I got into a fight, and beat this guy up pretty bad. The next morning Dad and I were just getting up and I had told him that I had to give a guy a whipping the night before. He smiled and with a little chuckle said, "I'm sure my definition of an ass whipping is different than yours." I tried to explain that I had beaten this guy up pretty bad, but he only dismissed it with a wave of his hand. Casey came by soon after the conversation and said, "I saw that guy you got into it with, and he looks bad." I asked him, "Where did you see him at?" And his reply was, "coming out of that church at the mouth of the hollow." Dad said, "Well, mine and your definitions may mean the same thing after all; anytime you get into a fight and the other guy finds religion then he took a bad one."

Even after my father's death I had men he had beaten up starting fights with me. The only reason I could think of was in some twisted way they thought beating me up would be getting back at my father or it would be some kind of redemption for them. Either way they just ended up with two ass whippings instead of one. Casey and I had gotten barred from every club within a hundred mile radius at least once, but the club nearest to us would always let us back in after a month or so. I thought I had to follow my father's footsteps, and was under the delusion that being a man was being tough. In reality I was only being an asshole. It didn't take long for me to realize I didn't want to have to fight every time I left the house. It had its appeal for a while, but when it got to the point I couldn't go to the grocery store without knowing if I was going to get in a fight or not, it was time to do something different.

Casey had a steady girlfriend and they had two children. It had been about a year since Crystal and I went our separate ways. So, I was kind of looking for a relationship if I could ever find the right person.

Chapter 17

I was setting at home watching a movie when out of the blue I get a call from my friend's girlfriend, Laura, whom I had met at the beach. She asked if I had seen Jordan or if he had been around. When I told her no, she asked if I had seen her boyfriend Josh. I figured out what was going on, because she knew damn well I hadn't seen her boyfriend, because he never came to my house. She asked, "What are you up to?" "Oh, just watching a movie," was my reply. She said, "That sounds nice." I told her, "Come on up; I just got back from the doctor we'll catch a buzz." She came up and we watched about five minutes of the movie before we ended up sleeping together. I felt kind of bad sleeping with my friend's girlfriend. I justified it by convincing myself that he would have done the same thing to me if given the chance. Laura came up a few more times, but I was always trying to put her off on one of my other friends. They all thought she was "the prettiest thing they ever saw." They couldn't figure out why I didn't latch on to her. I told her if she broke up with her boyfriend, we could start going out once everything cooled down. My friends kept hitting on her, but she kept turning them all down.

I decided to quit doing medication of every kind, but knew I couldn't get clean at my house or by myself. I asked my mother for help and I moved back home. I lost track of Laura for a couple months. I lay in bed sweating, shitting, throwing up, and hurting worse than I thought possible. There were nights when I woke up lying in a pool of sweat hurting so bad it was all I could do to lay a towel over it to try and soak it up. It was like the flu X 10 and it was like that for a month. Although after the first two weeks I started feeling like I just had the flu, minus the X 10. I was determined to quit and after a month of lying in bed doing nothing worthwhile or productive I started moving around. Laura found out where I was, and started calling again. After what I had been through it was nice to hear her soft sweet voice.

We started talking more and more, and it wasn't long before we were going out. On the first date I broke down, and we got high. After all the hell I just went through I was digging myself another hole. I was a little taken back by how beautiful she was after not seeing her for a while, and to tell you the truth I would probably jumped off a bridge if she would have suggested that instead. It wasn't like I put up much of a fight to tell the truth I was expecting and maybe even secretly hoping she would mention it.

Laura had grown up differently than I had. She was from a different class than I was used to, where everyone around the house was more, or less the "working class" variety sorta speak, Laura was from a well off wealthy family. Her mother didn't like the idea of her going out with me at first. She had grown up and went to school with all of my aunts and uncles. She knew the reputation my family had for not taking any shit, and I'm sure once she started asking around about me she found out I was cut from the same cloth. Laura's mother, however, was never rude nor did she try to talk down to me or bullshit me in anyway. I couldn't blame her for her concerns. She had worked very hard to put her daughter in the position to succeed and didn't want her being hindered by anyone or anything. Laura's father was also very kind and more down to earth than I expected. Even though her parents were divorced they got along very well.

Something I was not familiar with. I had heard about such things, but I thought they were about as real as fire breathing dragons.

Laura and I got along great and within four months decided to move in together. We lived together for three years and I never remember having what I would classify as an argument and only a handful of disagreements that were worked out or forgotten about in ten minutes. At least that was my impression. She was my best friend, and I thought I was hers but as the story goes on you will find out I was delusional. I was still going through physical therapy for the injury I sustained due to the rock falling on me while working in the mines. Laura started working for her mother's ex-boyfriend who more or less made a job for her to try and get back in the good graces of her mother. He was a good man none the less and Laura and I both liked him very much. He was a local land developer, a business he started with his brother.

His brother and his wife were constantly hitting on Laura. Writing her little notes that she use to bring home and show me. I couldn't believe some of the stuff that his wife was writing her. She said they would both say nasty comments whenever no one was around, and offered her money to sleep with them. I thought it was funny for a fifty something year old man and his twenty something year old wife to make advances to a girl that wasn't able to buy alcohol yet. She asked me what she should do because they were getting worse and bolder. Together we came up with four options. She could sue them for sexual harassment, and with the letters it would have been no problem to prove. She could tell her mother's ex and have him take care of it. She could play along, and take them for all she could before telling them to go to hell, or she could just continue to ignore it and hoped they got the picture and left her alone.

She didn't want to sue them because it would hurt her mother's ex, who had been so good to us just as bad as it would his brother. She chose to try and to continue to ignore it in the hopes they would leave her alone after about a month and them still giving her hell she told her mother's ex and he assured her he would take care of it and for a while they stopped. When they started back we decided if she wasn't going to sue them, that she was going to hustle them for all they were worth. I was on the verge of beating the shit out of him, but he was damn near sixty and knowing my luck he would have a heart attack and died. He was also apt to try to shoot me afterward. We went over how she was going to do it, what to say, and how to act, to string them along. At this time we had a two hundred dollar a day habit. That wasn't to get high that was just to get out of bed and be able to function.

Laura started bringing home five or six hundred dollars a week and telling me how she talked "the old pervert" out of it when he was hitting on her. As time went on the dollar amount was increasing. She would sometimes have as much as two or three thousand dollars. When I asked how she got it she would tell me a story about stealing it out of the safe or some other similar way. I knew her mother's ex was not stupid and if she stole it, it would soon be noticed. It had crossed my mind that she had succumbed to their advances but I put that thought out of my mind because I knew she loved me and would never do that. I trusted her completely. We were best friends and had been through a lot together. She was still coming up with an extra five hundred dollars or so every week and it was the same old story about hustling "the old pervert."

Eventually she and I decided to get clean. There was a new treatment that was very popular and effective that blocked the effects of opioids. No matter how much dope you did you couldn't get high. So, if you couldn't get high, then what was the point? It was a simple operation where they put an implant in her side after she went through a two day rapid detox. It was expensive but her mother's ex offered to pay for it if she would have it done. I on the other hand did it the old fashion way-cold turkey.

I had started back to work even though I didn't particularly like the coal mines. Actually, I hated it, but it paid well and it was a job I knew how to do. Every day when the heavy, never ending, dirty ass work started getting to me, it was the thought of providing a better life for Laura and myself that got me through. My dad's and my old friend, Donnie, is the one who had gotten me the job and since we only live a short distance apart, he and I rode to work together and split the cost. It was anywhere from a hour and a half to a two hour trip one way, it was just according to how bad the traffic was. We worked ten to twelve hour days six and sometimes even seven days a week. When you add three or four hours of driving there and take into account the hour it took to get the coal dirt off once you got home there wasn't enough time to sleep much less get high. It was not only a job it was also pulling double duty as rehab. I had quit taking pills to get high. The only time I took them is when my back hurt so bad I couldn't stand it and I needed them to be able to get through work or get to sleep. Donnie and I did, however, smoke at least one joint going to and coming from work every day. With two hours to kill, it made the drive not as monotonous.

Laura and I had both gotten straightened out and kicked the habit, for the first time since my father died I was looking forward to the future. I had been having trouble out of a tooth and Laura scheduled an appointment for me, but it was going to be several weeks before my dentist could get me in. This did give me time enough to let my boss know I was going to have to miss a day.

Chapter 18

Just as I was walking out of the door to go to my dental appointment, I got a frantic call from my mother saying, "Doc's house is on fire." As soon as the words came out of her mouth, I was out the door while telling her I would meet her there. When I arrived I saw two fire trucks, but only a few firemen. My mother was sitting on Doc's front lawn crying. Two people I didn't recognize were trying to console her. A guy I knew was trying to get a hose off the fire truck by himself. He finally yelled, "Charlie, help me get these hoses off here. I can't do it myself." He and I start pulling the hoses off; while another fireman connected them to the truck. After we had enough hose off the truck, I saw another fireman arrive, start dragging the hose close to the house and spraying the cause of all the smoke. I didn't see any flames, but the smoke was incredible.

My mother saw me as I finished helping get the hoses off the truck and called to me saying, "Doc's still in the house." When she told me that, I ran into the house and up the stairs. Doc's bedroom was on the second floor. Despite the fact he used a wheel chair to get around. I only made it to the first landing before I was overcome by the smoke. I managed to make it back outside, coughing and blinded by the smoke. Once I was back outside and started to get my senses back, I heard mom begging and arguing with the fire fighters to, "go get Doc, or give me a mask and I'll go myself."

While all of this was going on, back at the office Doc's accountant was calling in prescriptions of Xanax. This same accountant was supposed to have taken Doc his breakfast at 9:00 a.m. The fire was noticed well after 10:00 a.m. and she still hadn't taken him his breakfast, even though the secretary had brought it to her at 9:00 am as planned. The Doctor's office and the pharmacy are side by side. When the pharmacist heard a strange voice from the doctor's office trying to get a prescription filled (while the doctor's house was burning to the ground), she immediately called the police. When Doc's estranged wife arrived to see that the office was properly shut down and medical records taken care of, she was confronted by the accountant. She refused to give his wife the keys to the back room where the prescription pads were, or to leave so she could lock the office up until she could get a hold of the proper people to come and deal with the patient records. His wife had to call the police: she was told an officer was on his way and he would be notified of the additional problem.

The policeman who showed up was having an affair with the accountant and had even fathered her twin girls, all the while still being married to someone else. It is only common sense to think that after he swept the prescription fraud under one rug he would sweep any other crime she may have committed under another. If this guy would go home and lie to his wife every night after he had left his mistress and cover up one crime, how could he be believed or trusted?

Doc was believed to have dirt on all of the political figures and most law enforcement in McDowell County, along with a good portion in and around the state. After Doc's house was cleared of firefighters and smoke, the police and others who had an interest in finding "the hidden records" they all believed he had, they started their "investigation." For two days they went through every nook and cranny of Doc's house searching for those files. They knew those records had to be somewhere and if they were found by the wrong people, a lot of people would be in a lot of trouble. The day after Doc's death they woke my mother up and had her come to Doc's house at 3:00 a.m. to open Doc's safe. They were certain Doc kept the "little black book" hidden there. Mom said there were people there that had nothing to do with law enforcement walking around Doc's house pretending to look busy as she opened the safe. Mom found out later that they had called Doc's wife before they called her asking about the combination, but she told them, "If Betty doesn't know it, then no one does." Mom called and told me about it saying, "I know they are looking for all the records doc was supposed to have on all of them; but they will never find them." After days of searching and not finding what they were looking for, they were all in agreement that they had to be at his office.

They then moved the search to his office. They went through thousands of patient's files, thinking he may have hidden them under someone's name that had passed away or didn't exist. They looked for days and had begun boxing up medical records that were protected under the HIPPA act that protects patient's privacy. Every one of those county police had violated Federal Law hundreds of times in the past few days, but was too stupid to know or care. By this time the State Police were getting curious as to what was going on and wanted to see what kept the sheriff's office there at all hours of the night. When they saw them going through medical records, talking and telling one another who was sick and what they were suffering from, they told them they had committed a federal crime and explained to them what the HIPPA Act was. When questioned about what they were doing over at the office when the fire was at Doc's house, they had no answer. They told the sheriff's office that "this is your baby" and they didn't want any part of it.

Once they figured out they were now subject to criminal charges themselves, they had to come up with a plan. If they could get the fire marshal to say he believed it was arson and not an accidental fire then maybe, just maybe, that would over shadow any indiscretions they had committed. They ended up talking the younger Fire Marshal into saying what they wanted him to say. When they did the older of the two fell right into place, even though they knew the insurance investigator said the cause of the fire was undetermined and had paid the insurance policy off as such. They knew they now had a chance of getting by with looking through patient's protected personal records that could only legally be examined by someone appointed by a federal judge or if they were released by the patients themselves. Here was the crooked, lying cops of McDowell County breaking more laws than the people they were putting in jail and getting by with it. As soon as someone started questioning or suspecting something was not quite right with the whole "arson" theory, they would come up with another piece of Perry Mason "evidence". Real gumshoes: those deputies.

I went back home the evening after the fire and phoned Laura to tell her what had happened. She had quit work and was going back to school to get a nursing degree. Since her college was a two hour drive from where we lived, she spent two nights a week at her mom's-who lived only a few miles from the college. Even though I did miss going to bed with her, the truth is, I was usually asleep as soon as my head touched the pillow. So I hardly noticed if she was there or not. That is until I got up alone the next morning.

Chapter 19

Everything was going well. We were both clean, work was getting easier and Laura's summer break was coming up soon. My work said they were going to try and cut us back to eight hour days. So when Laura's break did come up we would be able to spend some time together. We hadn't been able to do much of anything together since I started back to work.

I had just finished everything I needed in preparation for the next shift that was coming on. I was monitoring the belt for any larger than usual rock that may have gotten stuck between the belt and top (ceiling of mine). If that happens and it's not immediately dislodged, it can damage or break the belt that could keep me there all night trying to get the belt back online. It was 3:30 in the afternoon and quitting time was at 5:00. I didn't want anything keeping me longer than necessary. It was Friday and payday. Laura was coming back from staying with her mother and we were going to celebrate the rare occurrence of my two day weekend.

I was kicked back watching and listening to the roar of the belt when I heard the phone sound off. Phones inside of the coal mines do not ring; they have a loud horn that can be heard above the noise of normal everyday operations. They were also setup as an open line, similar to the phones back in the 40's and 50's. When the phone sounds off, anyone who hears it goes to answer it to see who it is for or if it concerns their part of the mine.

I hear the outside man and someone farther up the line talking. The outside man is saying, "There are four police cars coming up the hill as we speak" and the other replies," Tell them I didn't show up for work today." After a pause I hear the outside man tell him he was only joking; after which he was cursed with words I had never heard before. I thought it served him right. To play such a joke on a man was bad enough, but to do it on payday was enough to cause a fight. I sat there for another hour watching the belt, day dreaming, and planning my weekend when the electrician pulls in. He tells me that he needs me to go outside with him and help him change the motor in one of the rides. I told him it was 4:30 and I was not moving for another thirty minutes and then it was not going to be to help him change a motor. I was going home. I had been tricked into doing that shit before, only to spend half the night doing something I didn't want to do in the first place. I was picking up my check and enjoying my two days off. When he saw this line wasn't working; he then told me what his true intentions were.

He told me, "There are police crawling around everywhere and the boss man told me to come and get you. He told me not to let you know the police were waiting on you. He said he was afraid you wouldn't come out and the police would shut him down while they searched the mine for you." At first I didn't believe him and explained to him that it was payday and I wasn't in the mood to be played with especially about shit like that. He went on telling me how serious he was, swearing he wasn't lying. By this time I was getting pissed off. I told him that I had already overheard another guy talking to the outside man. He told me that the boss told him to say he was joking in case you were listening. I will never forget his face and how he looked at me. His eyes were open wide and brows arched. He had a slight frown that looked like it would have been painful for him to open his mouth. He was taking a pill bottle out of his pocket as he spoke saying, "Listen to what I'm telling you. The police are outside waiting on you and I was told to come and get you." He opened the bottle and told me to hold out my hand and he poured six pills in my hand. He said, "Here are six Lortabs. Do you want to snort them or eat them before you go to jail?" It was like he was giving me the pills to ease his pain for having to tell me I was going to jail, more than to ease mine for having to go. I grabbed the water bottle I had been drinking from and tossed the pills in my mouth knowing he wasn't trying to pull a prank. I hadn't took pills in a while but if I was going to jail, I figured it best to try and minimize as much of the pain as possible while I still had an option.

I got my dinner bucket and hopped in his ride telling him, "Let's go and get this over with." On the ride out I kept running it over and over in my head trying to figure out what they could want with me. I had gotten into a fight a couple weeks before, and the guy I was fighting with took a bad one so I suspected it had something to do with that. We got within five breaks of the outside (200 feet) and the electrician stopped and placed one hand on my shoulder while pointing with the other saying, "I feel bad about lying to you back there. Right there is the return you can slip out that way and I'll tell them I couldn't find you." I told him I appreciated it, but whatever they had me charged with was bullshit and if I went now I could post bond when the magistrate came in at 10:00 p.m. and be back to work Monday and avoid having to stay all weekend in jail. I did tell him, "When we clear the drift mouth, I'm going to get off; you go on back to the shed and park the ride like you would normally do, that way they won't suspect you told me anything." We shook hands and he told me "good luck."

Once we cleared the entrance it took my eyes a second to adjust to the daylight. As I was regaining focus, I could see the police trying to hide behind cars and the mining equipment that had become a permanent fixture around the mine. They looked ridiculous. As the ride stopped and I stepped off, I told them to "come on out, you all look silly trying to hide like that." There were at least six of them that came at me with their guns drawn, yelling for me to put my hands up. I asked, "Why don't you all get a real job. I heard McDonald's was hiring. Then you could at least say you worked for a living." They were telling me to take off my mining light, belt, and hat. I went about it at my own pace, asking them, "What do you mother fuckers want with me," and, of course I, got a smartass response after I was handcuffed by one of the Boone County Sherriff's Deputies. He said," Parking ticket asshole." I went on to tell him how stupid he sounded; that McDowell County wouldn't come all that way over traffic tickets. That's when one of the McDowell County Deputy's that I knew stepped in. I had gone to school with his son and I had knew for a fact that he was giving pills to the dope whores who lived around him in exchange for sex. He knew that I knew, so when he stepped up he was more down to earth; probably because he was afraid I was going to tell his little secret to all his cop buddies. That's when he told me, I was being arrested for murder. "Who was I supposed to have killed?" I asked, thinking he was bullshitting me. He told me "Doc" and then I knew he was serious, but I had trouble believing anyone would think I would try and hurt Doc. I must have been in shock, because my mind wasn't registering the gravity of the situation.

Chapter 20

I was first taken to the Boone County Court House, where the magistrate released me into the custody of the McDowell County deputies. On the way back to McDowell County I noticed they were taking their time. I asked if they would mind speeding up. They came back with one of their usual smartass answers asking, "Are you in a hurry to go to jail?" I said, "No, I just don't want to miss the magistrate when he comes in tonight." They told me that only a circuit judge could set a bond for murder and it would be two weeks before I would have a hearing. That's when the weight and severity of the charges I was facing started sinking in. They went on to tell me that they knew I didn't have anything to do with it, but they believed I knew who did: that the best thing for me to do was to come clean. Once they started that bullshit I lost all control. I cursed them, their mother, cousins, and kids. I screamed, yelled, and talked so much shit by the time I got to the court house I had lost my voice. When I got out of the car it looked like a bucket of coal had exploded in the back of his car. When they arrested me I was still in my mining boots and coveralls. I was filthy from working all day and had tried my best to give that cop something to do later on. At the least he may finally earn his pay for a change. When they saw the mess I made, the cop who was just along for the ride started picking at the guy who owned the car. The owner of the car kept saying that he hoped I enjoyed prison and a few other smartass comments, but I knew I would have the last laugh. So after they got me to the sheriff's station, he said he was leaving to go clean his car. As he was walking out the door I said, "You remember that comment you made about me enjoying prison? Well, enjoy cleaning up my mess." I watched as his ears turned red. He started to come back inside the station but thought better of it and left.

I was finger printed, moved to a little room in the back and interrogated. I didn't have an answer for most of their questions. I had no clue what they were asking me about. There were questions about Doc's house, not about any kind of arson or murder. I was confused to say the least. Even if I wanted to help them, I couldn't. Eventually they did get around to asking me about Casey. When was the last time I saw him and if I thought he was capable of murder. I told them it had been a few months since I last saw Casey, and if they were insinuating Casey killed Doc, "Why would he?" I told them as far as I know; Casey and Doc had no relationship. I was starting to put it together now. I was the only connection Casey would have to Doc other than him going to Doc for medical treatment for an injury or illness. I explained to them that they were barking up the wrong tree if they thought Casey and I killed Doc.

The sheriff's deputies left and returned a few minutes later, but this time they were accompanied by a big round - headed cop who said he was a member of the Drug and Violent Crime Task Force. He was bald, overweight, and had a sickening stench of french fries mixed with body odor. He began asking me about my mother's relationship with Doc. I told him what anyone else that knew them could have told him. She worked for Doc for the past twenty-five years; she took care of him, and was at his beck and call. Doc had a bad habit of calling her at all hours of the night for some kind of political nonsense that could easily have waited until the next day. He asked about their being romantically involved and I told him I didn't think they were; that he would have to ask her. That's when his attitude changed and he started screaming about Doc sleeping with her. When he didn't get the response he was looking for he brought Laura into Doc's sexual conquests. I reminded him how pathetic he sounded and he started saying, "I just fucked your mother and Laura and they were both begging me for it." He also went on to say some other nasty shit that isn't fit to be repeated much less printed. I let him know how childish and transparent his performance was. That it made me question his ability and this so called "Drug and Violent Crime Task Force". He soon had enough and told the Sherriff's Deputy's to "take this smartass to jail."

The County jail was next door to the police station and was only a temporary holding facility for people who had been arrested, but not convicted of a crime. I was told the following day that I would be transported to the regional jail when the next "bus" ran. I was awakened in the middle of the night by a CO saying there was a deputy that needed to speak with me and that it was "urgent." The first thing that came to my mind was they had made a mistake and was going to drop the charges or something similar to that. I was taken to an interrogation room where the cop said to me, "You can help yourself out tremendously if you can find out where the files and other records Doc has been keeping on everyone for the past twenty years are." I told him I would do what I could, but I would have to be able to talk to mom face to face or she wouldn't tell me anything. He said he would be back before they took me to the regional jail the next evening. I needed to find something out quick.

I was up the next morning bright and early, calling mom telling her that I needed to speak to her face to face. She said she would use her political connections to see what she could do. Eventually she was able to secure a thirty minute visit at 1:00 p.m. I'm sure the police had something to do with me being allowed to see her. They wanted those files so badly; they would probably have agreed to anything, but I didn't know it at the time.

When my mother got there at 1:00, I could tell she had gotten little if any sleep and that she had been crying. It broke my heart to see her in such a vulnerable state. She was much stronger than I was and if she couldn't keep it together - how could I? We were put into the same interrogation room I had been in at 2:00 am. the night before when I was summoned by the Sherriff's deputy. I thought it wasn't a coincidence and gave the room a quick search looking for recording devices. Even though I didn't find any, that didn't mean there weren't any. Hell, I wouldn't know what a bug looked like anyway. We only had thirty minutes and I wasn't going to waste it. We spoke to one another in low voices and, in some instances, even whispered into one another's ear. She asked me what was going on and I told her all I knew. Casey and I were suspected of starting the fire at Doc's house, and that was it. I also relayed to her the same questions the police had asked me about Doc's house and about being awakened in the middle of the night by the deputy and him telling me I could tremendously help my situation if I could find out where Doc had those files he kept on everyone. Mom said, "That's why they were asking you about Doc's house. They think they had missed or overlooked something." That something being the hiding spot or whereabouts of those records. She told me in a voice louder than I was comfortable with, "They will never find them." I told her to keep it down and asked her point blank where they were. She told me that if she told me, "You can never tell a soul." She got closer than usual and whispered so low

I could barely understand her. She told me the secret Doc and she had been keeping since shortly after she started working for him. That for over what had to be twenty years her and Doc had been acting like he was keeping files and recording anyone who was anyone: especially political officials and law enforcement. They would say things to one another in the presence of certain people who had a habit of saying too much or gossiping that "We've got to put that in the file" or if Doc was on the phone he would ask her "Did you record that?" She said he had fake phone lines ran into dresser drawers or into the next room. Whenever he had company over, they would tell others he was recording his phone calls. That was how he got things done that no one else was able to. He only had to repeat what he knew of their wrong-doing or hint to a phone call they had sometimes years earlier, and his wish was their command. "The truth is there are no files or records!" She said out of all of the things Doc told her the most valuable was, "Just because the files don't exist doesn't mean they aren't real. To everyone but us they are real, because they believe they are."

When the deputy returned to see if I had learned the location of the records from my mom, I told him I wanted to see my attorney. I had nothing to say unless my attorney was present.

Chapter 21

The regional jail was pretty much what I expected. I had a hard time at first trying to make sense of what was going on. Laura and my mother were coming up to the jail to see me as much as possible. The three of us knew nothing of what was going on, but Mom tried to explain things as she understood them to be. My being in jail was taking a toll on my mom, but she never complained.

I took comfort in knowing Laura would be okay for a month or so. She had the paycheck I wasn't able to get the day of my arrest and I had another one coming in two weeks. I advised her to get caught up on the bills and use the money wisely, in case it took me a while to make bond once it had been set.

At my preliminary hearing I was anxious to see the evidence they had to support their claim I had murdered Doc. I had been assigned an attorney, but had only met with him one time. I was surprised on the day of my preliminary hearing that a different attorney was present. The new lawyer told me he was sent by my attorney. I was not happy to say the least, but I went over what I wanted him to say and ask. Before I could get it all out he tells me that, "We will be waiving your preliminary hearing." My response to that was, "Like hell we are." I argued with this guy for thirty minutes trying to make him understand the word innocent. I was adamant about having my prelim, until he recruited my mother in assisting him in his argument. I waived my hearing after I had spoken to my mother; even though I knew I shouldn't have.

My mother had spoken to my attorney: he was confident that I would be given a bond, although he didn't know how much it would be. He said he would be afraid to guess or at least that's what he told her. I had to go in front of the circuit judge five different times in as many months before a bond was set.

After the first month Laura was not staying at the house anymore. She was staying at her mother's and I feared she had given up on me. Something was going on. She had written to me and told me she was working at Hooters. I wasn't pleased to say the least, but she had to take care of herself while I was in jail. So, what could I really say? My cousin, Kenneth, had a friend who went to the same school as she did. I asked Kenneth if he would ask his friend to stop by her work and check on her. I hadn't been able to get in touch with her on the phone and hadn't gotten any mail in over two weeks. Coincidentally, Kenneth's friend came over that weekend and Kenneth asked him for the favor and showed him a picture of the two of us.

In less than a week I got a letter from Kenneth telling me to call him. When I called he told me what he was able to find out. His friend went to Laura's work and saw her just as she was getting off. He saw her leaving with her father, or maybe, her grandfather. At least that was what he thought, until they got into the car where "she kissed him like no girl would a family member." Damn, even now that's a hard pill to swallow. What made matters worse is that "old pervert" line she was constantly using, was just that-a line. She used it to cover up what she was really doing. Her screwing "old men" was bad enough, but when I look back I should have seen it coming. I trusted her with all my heart and she used that to her advantage and to make me believe her lies. Wow!! It was so nasty that I still have trouble believing it. Could she really have a thing for these "old men," or was she just a money grubbing whore, with no morals or sense of self- worth?

When I did get in touch with her, it was over the phone. She was all lovey dovey, and acted like everything was ok. That was until I asked her about the "old man" she was seen kissing. She started crying, telling me how much she loved me and how hard it was on her, me not being there. I couldn't figure out if she was genuinely sorry, or if she was ashamed of herself for screwing "old men" along with lying and cheating. Never- the- less that was my last conversation with her.

The judge set my bond at two hundred and fifty thousand dollars, with the stipulation that I was to be fitted with an ankle monitor and confined to home. I was not allowed to work or leave my home for any reason other than to go for scheduled appointments with my attorney or doctor. I could, however, go to church, but only for Sunday morning service. I was on home confinement for fifteen months and never had a problem. Kenneth's younger brother was mad about something small and inconsequential and called my home confinement officer. He told her that I had stolen his car. Because I had an ankle monitor on she knew exactly where I was. My cousin should have known she had caller I.D. As soon as she told me the number, I knew exactly who it was.

I tried to help my attorney as much as I could. I was ignorant of the rules, laws and procedures or what to expect at trial, but I did my best. I had never been through anything like this before: some speeding tickets were the extent of my knowledge of the justice system. During those fifteen months of home confinement, I did find out what evidence they had. Casey and I went to high school with a guy by the name of Mike Miller. Mike went to my attorney's office several months after I was arrested and told him how the Sherriff's Deputy had picked him up a few weeks after Doc's death. The cops took him to three different police stations in the course of a ten hour period. He said that they had slapped, punched, and threatened to put him in jail because of a few bad checks he had written. They kept saying they knew he dropped Casey and I off that morning. After eight hours of torture, he gave in and said what the police told him to say. He went on to say the police told him not only what to say, but also how to act: "when we record you, you have to be calm or it won't be convincing." They told him where and what time he was supposed to have picked us up and dropped us off. Mike told my attorney that for eight hours he told the police he didn't know anything and hadn't laid eyes on me for months. Mike went on to explain to my attorney that while this was going on he was getting sicker and sicker from not having "a pill" and that he was hurting so bad that he would have told them anything to get out of there so he could get a "fix."

That was how the police obtained their arrest warrant. I guess they figured once they had me, I would find out from mom where Doc's "secret files and records" were. Once they had that piece of information, they could drop the charges. No harm no foul. Since I couldn't give them fictional "records," I was stuck. If I told them the records didn't exist, they wouldn't have believed me anyway. They kept putting pressure on mom through me, thinking she would eventually give them up. I also learned the state was going to be allowed to use a fight Casey and I had gotten into a few years earlier. They planned to use this info against

Casey and me even though it had nothing to do with what we were charged with.

The cops went as far as recruiting jail house snitches: one for Casey, the other for me. Both of whom were cell mates and were given deals to get out of jail if they would testify. Casey had gotten into a fist fight with his rat. The fight, however, was long before all of the testifying talk and they had nothing to do with one another. It did, however, give him motive to do what he did. Well, that and freedom. It was killing two birds with one stone. Their testimonies did not match up to what the police and medical examiner said happened. They looked pathetic, rather than like credible witnesses. I was surprised that the state would use such idiots, but use them they did.

Other than the two idiot "rats" and a recanting witness, they had absolutely no evidence on Casey or me. It wasn't long before they started bringing my mother into their pathetic story.

Two people could account for my where abouts the morning before the fire. My neighbor saw me go to my truck that morning to get a pack of cigarettes I had in the glove compartment. I had just gotten out of bed. I was barefooted and had nothing on but a pair of shorts. My neighbor even told me "good morning." I had also spoken to Laura around 8:00 that morning for what was easily thirty minutes before she had to go so she could make it to class on time.

The days prior to the trial I wasn't worried at all. I was actually confident and couldn't wait to get the whole misunderstanding behind me. The one thing that truly bothered me, was that at the last pretrial hearing my attorney "let it slip" about Mike recanting. He told the prosecutor two weeks before trial that Mike Miller, the state's only witness was going to recant the statement he made. He even went on to tell them he was going to tell about the "eight hours of torture" he had endured at the hands of the Deputy Sheriff. Outside in the hallway, he told me he was "sorry" that he let his emotions get the better of him and he should have never said anything.

When the Prosecuting Attorney told the Deputies what he had learned, they immediately went to find their star witness. When he found out the police were looking for him, he went into hiding and didn't come out until the trial. My attorney had sworn to him that he wouldn't say anything to anybody about him going to tell the truth at trial. My attorney not only broke his confidence, but he also gave the prosecuting attorney two weeks to prepare for what should have been something shocking and unexpected. The State now had a chance to minimize the damage and prepare.

Chapter 22

The trial began with the Prosecutor's opening argument. These were the first words out of his mouth. "You're not going to hear about a lot of physical evidence in this case. What you are going to hear is a lot of circumstantial evidence. They say circumstantial evidence is not good evidence, but if your driveway is not wet before you go to bed, and when you wake up it is; its circumstantial evidence that it rained while you were sleeping." He went on dancing around proof and evidence for another twenty minutes.

My attorney answered the State's analogy with a half-hearted remark saying, "The drive way could have gotten wet by a number of other ways. A neighbor while watering his hedges may have gotten it wet, or the sprinklers could have gone off before you woke up, and it got wet that way." He said a few other things I can't quite remember, but I know it must have been so bad that I repressed the memory in hopes of not having to relive that nightmare ever again.

For the most part I can only describe the trial as excruciating. To sit there and not be able to respond or show any type of emotion was tough. It was truly unbelievable the bare face lies that were told during the course of my trial; it was almost more than I could bear. I had to depend on my attorney to do the talking for me. I had been slightly aware of a little bit of a stutter my attorney had, but I didn't think it was something that I needed to be concerned with. What I didn't know was the more excited and nervous he became, the more pronounced his stuttering was. When your life depends on your attorney's ability to convey a certain message and refute the picture the state is trying to paint, you do not want a stu-stuttering attorney. Take my word for it!

Presenting facts or evidence was not in the Prosecutor's game plan. He focused his assault on my mother and her relationship with Doc. It was so bad; I started thinking everyone had forgotten I was the one on trial. Not my mother. I felt like jumping up, waving my arms, and screaming, "Here I am."

The State called Mike Miller their "star witness" and he did exactly what he said he was going to do. He told the truth. The judge did, however, allow the prosecutor to replay the original statement Mike had made. It was incredible to hear him tell such a story. There was no way the police made up the story he was telling on the spot. It was too detailed and well thought out. Despite the fact Mike told the jury everything he said about me was a lie, it was still damaging.

We did learn that the Circuit Clerk tried to call Mike several times while he was hiding. He did talk to Mike's mother and told her she needed to "talk to Mike and tell him that if he changes his story now, it will not only be bad for him, but for his whole family." The prosecutor admitted to asking the Circuit Clerk to call and speak with Mike. He said, "I had some concerns about his testimony, and since the deputy was unable to get in contact with him, I asked Mr. Crooks (Circuit Clerk) if he would mind calling to see if he had better luck getting in touch with him."

Laura didn't show up to testify. I guess her "old man" wouldn't let her come. My attorney didn't subpoena her and I was ignorant to the fact that he could have. If he did she would have had no other choice but to come. My neighbor came through. He told the jury he had talked to me that morning a little before 8:00. He told them that he could tell I had just gotten out of bed and all I had on was a pair of shorts.

The Fire Marshal said that in his opinion, the fire started between 7:30 a.m. and 8:00 a.m. There was no way I could have been anywhere near Doc's house if I was home when the fire marshal said the fire started. Doc's house was right beside the main road. There is no way I could have escaped detection by someone either going to or coming from his house during the peak times people were going to work. It would have taken longer than thirty minutes to get there, much less back. It's a thirty minute drive one way, and that's if there is no traffic at all, and I would still need time to break in and start the fire. How would I have gotten home if Mike had dropped me off? I tried to get my attorney to make up a time line of the events the State claimed happened. I wanted him to make a timeline of what had actually happened and could be corroborated. He could present them both to the jury and they could compare the evidence as presented. He wouldn't hear of it. I tried to make one myself, but he had all of the statements and files. I didn't know if I was allowed to have them or not, and was too ignorant of the law to ask for them.

The State brought up the fight Casey and I had gotten into. When the witnesses took the stand, they said they didn't hold a grudge; it was just one of those things. It was over and forgotten. Even though their testimony wasn't as bad as the Prosecutor had hoped, it still showed Casey and I were capable of violence. It had absolutely nothing to do with arson; so I guess it was a way for the judge to pay Doc back for all those years of political support.

The adulterous police officer, Don Beavers, was a real piece of work. Either he, the Prosecutor, or both made up a fictional character that they referred to as a "confidential informant." The purpose of this "confidential informant" was to substantiate the statement the police had coached Mike through. When my attorney asked who the "confidential informant" was, the Prosecutor said they wanted to remain anonymous, and he wouldn't release their name. My attorney tried to explain to him that I had a constitutional right to face my accuser. If someone saw Mike that morning, it should have been revealed to us in discovery. Especially if this "confidential informant" said they saw Mike drop Casey and I off at Doc's office the morning of the fire. He asked the deputy, "Did it ever occur to you that this 'confidential informant' may be lying, or that he may have had information he didn't realize he had that would prove Mr. Pangloss' innocence? If we don't know who he or she is, how are we to know one way or the other?" Deputy Beavers answer to this was, "I told you what they told me." My attorney went on to ask the deputy what Casey and I were wearing that morning and exactly where in the parking lot where we dropped off." To both questions the deputy said he didn't know. "So, you're saying all we have to prove what this 'confidential informant' said is what you said they said, and the only proof that we have that this person even exists is your word?" After my attorney asked this last question I will never forget the smug look Deputy Beavers had on his face when he said, "That's right, my word!" Neither my attorney, nor the judge said anything. The Prosecutor on redirect did ask if it was "common practice" to use "confidential informants." As you could have guessed, Deputy Beavers said it was. When questioned further and asked to name just one other trial where a confidential informant was used and their identity never revealed or mentioned until the trial, Deputy Beavers said he could not and my attorney ended his redirect by saying, "The reason why Mr. Beavers can't name just one case is because it's a violation of the constitution and doesn't happen".

The trial lasted longer than anticipated. The week was over and the weekend had started. The judge instructed us all to be back at 9:00 Monday morning, and the attorneys to be ready to present their closing arguments. Before we left the judge asked if there was any more business that needed taken care of before we recessed for the weekend. The Prosecutor told the court that the State would like to drop the conspiracy charge. I couldn't believe what I was hearing. How could he use all of that made up evidence under the pretext of Casey and me working together? The judge had allowed the evidence and the jury was presented with testimony that had absolutely nothing to do with arson and definitely not murder.

After having to sit through a week of the Prosecutor portraying me as heartless, without actually saying it, was about more than I could endure. Between misleading statements and my stuttering lawyer, the week-end was a welcome change. I was physically and mentally spent. The more I thought about what was said during the course of the trial and how I was portrayed the less certain I became of being acquitted. I can't say I was doubting acquittal, but I wasn't as confident.

As soon as I was home I began drinking and getting high. I was trying to forget the past week, and my troubles. My cousin, Jessie, came to see me. He was the one person I knew I could trust and tell anything to. We went for a ride and I asked him to take me to where my father was buried. I figured if there was a possibility of never getting to see him again, I had better say my goodbyes-while I had the chance. This is also where we had spent our childhood together and rode our ponies; which now seemed like a life time ago. We laughed, cried, and bonded like only two brothers could. It was late Saturday night and we were setting in the truck with the heater running. Jess looked at me and asked, "Do you think you're going to get out of this?" My response was, "I didn't do anything wrong," and asked, "How can I know what someone else is thinking?" "It's impossible to prove I was anywhere near Doc's house that morning and I'll have to put my faith in that."

Jess turned the car off and took the keys out of the ignition. He leaned over, unlocked the glove box, and removed a wad of money. It was folded, but because it was so thick it looked more like it was rolled over with a rubber band wrapped around it. He said while holding the money out to me. "Here is $5,000.00. It's all I could come up with. If you think you're going to be found guilty, take it and get lost. I'll drop you wherever you want to be dropped off." I told him, "I can't be 100% for certain that I'll be found not guilty, but I am certain I can't run for the rest of my life." I don't know how Jess came up with that much money, but I know he had to have gone in debt to do it. He never put himself above the chance to do a kind act or to show his heart and selflessness. How many people know someone like that? Much less someone who would put themselves out, without being asked. He did it on the off chance I may have needed it. It felt like something reached in and squeezed my heart. The kicker was he never expected anything in return or to be repaid.

Jess and I continued to drink and reminisce until Sunday evening. He had to go to work the next day and I had to go to court. As I was lying there half drunk and completely high, my mind wouldn't shut down. I had not been to sleep since Thursday. I was eight hours away from court, and what was the most life changing event of my life, and I couldn't go to sleep. I laid there all night in the dark with my mind racing thinking about the what if's. Before I knew it, it was time to get up and go to court.

When I got to the court house my mind and thoughts were all over the place. I couldn't concentrate on anything. I felt sick and confused. When the final arguments got underway the tension seemed to vanish and a sense of calm came over me. I can't explain it really. I think I had been so wound up and worried about the final arguments that once they were underway, all that tension was released and I could catch my breath. I knew it would soon be over. When the prosecutor began his summation, I could hardly hold my eyes open. Not sleeping for the three days leading up to the final arguments began to catch up with me. I did everything I could to keep my eyes open, but I had no control. I bit my lip until it bled, but it only woke me for a second. My mind was conscious of everything going on around me, but no matter how much I struggled to keep my eyes open I still nodded off.

The jury deliberated for five days. On the fifth day I stood there facing the jury- waiting to hear my fate. I was confident I was going to hear them say not guilty. There was no evidence of arson or that I was even within twenty miles of Doc's house that morning. If there was no arson then there can't be a murder. So when the jury came back with the verdict of "Guilty", I thought I heard them wrong. I was stuck; frozen in that moment, unable to snap back to reality:

until the lights went off and everyone decided to put their hands on me. The lights were only off for maybe five seconds, but during that time the world came to a stop. You could have heard a pin drop, but when the lights came back on it was like someone pressed the play button for life to resume. Everyone commenced doing what they were five seconds before. I guess they expected me to do something when the light went off, but what could I have done? I said goodbye to my mother and aunt who were seated directly behind me. Then I was lead to a holding cell where I awaited transport to the regional jail.

Chapter 23

When I first arrived at the regional jail, I was stripped searched. My clothes and other belongings were taken and logged into what I was told was the "personal property storage." I was given two pairs of what resembled nursing scrubs only they were orange, two towels, two washcloths, three pairs of socks, three pairs of green underwear (briefs), one pair of orange shoes, and a laundry bag: all of which were previously worn, and damn near worn out. I reluctantly put on the clothing and put the rest in the laundry bag. The CO's escorted me to have my picture and fingerprints taken and recorded. I only had a few tattoos and scars, so it didn't take them long to photograph them. I was then taken to the nurse's station and given a quick once over. The process was simplified due to the fact I had been there before. I was then led down the hall. Once we went through several sliding doors, I came to what was going to be my new home for the next couple of years. Beside the door was a mat. I was told to take it with me: that it was mine. It was ripped, torn, and dirty, but what choice did I have? At this point I was a robot doing what I was told. My mind, feelings, and opinions were shut down. It was too much, too fast!

I was placed in a pod with 16 cells and 25 men. I was given a single cell because of the severity of my charge. I also assumed no one wanted to bunk with a convicted murderer. It was November 21 and I didn't have to wait long until I found out how it felt to spend Thanksgiving and Christmas alone and in jail. The Christmas holiday had always been very special to me as a child. I would wake my mother up every Christmas morning at four or five o'clock to open presents. I did this all the way up into my early twenties. Needless to say the first couple months were rough. It took a few months to get into the swing of things.

The first thing I took notice of was the prisoners who thought they were cool or tough constantly talking about how much money they made and had. Their conversations were mostly about all of the drugs they had sold or did. It must have been mandatory to have a pair of Timberland boots or Jordan shoes in their personal property, along with a two thousand dollar watch and a five thousand dollar chain. The thing I really found odd was their nick names: most of which they gave to themselves. I didn't even know you could give yourself a nickname. I thought it had to be given to you by someone else, but what do I know? All of these "nicknames" had some sort of reference to drugs or money. Some of my favorites are Key-Low, C-Note, Stacks, and Dollar. What was really ironic was most of them with these fancy "nicknames" couldn't buy a postage stamp.

The world is turned upside down in jail. The one constant is rapist and child molesters are the lowest of the low. They get spit on, talked shit to and beaten up almost everywhere they go. Every once in a while someone would vouch for one of them and they would be allowed to live in the pod and not be harassed. The majority of the time they would have to be put into P.C. (protective custody) or suffer constant insults and beatings. The most respected of the prisoners were those convicted of more violent crimes. They are the ones with the most influence, especially murderers. Everyone knew that jail, and eventually prison, was going to be their homes for a long time, if not forever. For the most part they were treated with a higher degree of respect. Fear plays a major role, and factors into who is respected and the amount of respect given. Well, that, and along with what crime they were convicted of. It's reasonable for people to think that if someone is in jail for murder, they have killed and are capable of killing again.

I was the one who everybody seemed to come to for advice. I tried to keep their best interests in mind. My advice was centered on them getting out of jail and keeping that their main focus and goal. I was objective and open minded. I didn't try to make a lot of friends, but I was friendly. Eventually I was able to get a few of the prisoners I knew moved into the same pod as myself and two of my closest friends. Both were in for murder as well. So, we had a common bond and were going to be together for a while. Under different circumstances, I would have been friends with both of them if I had met them on the street.

Dotson was 20 years old and the younger of the two. He was quiet and artistic. He was always drawing or making something. He had a little girl and she was cute as a button. He and I would schedule our visits at the same time. That way our families could meet and have each other to talk to while they waited to see us. His little girl had gotten used to seeing my mother and I. She was so sweet and after a while she overcame her shyness. She would talk to me and give me a hug whenever she saw me. Seeing that precious little girl so happy to see her dad, tugged on my heart. She didn't know or care where he was or why he was there. It broke my heart, but at the same time it was a beautiful thing to see unconditional love.

Like I had said before Dotson was constantly drawing or making something. He's the one who did the majority of my tattoos. We didn't have much to work with as far as tattoo supplies. There were no motors for tattoo guns or ink in the regional jail. We used a sharpened staple for the needle and melted it into the end of an ink pen or tooth brush for a handle. That was our "Tattoo gun" minus the gun. It was more like a stick with a needle on the end of it. Making the ink was a lot of work, but it was the most intriguing and educational. To start with, he would have to burn checkers or chess pieces. Any kind of plastic would work, but these two worked the best. He would also burn pomade. He would twist a piece of toilet paper up really tight and coat it with pomade. When lit it burns like a wick. He would stick this wick in the jar of pomade and light it. Dotson would make these paper cylinders to catch the smoke. Once the plastic or pomade started smoking he would catch it in the cylinder and what stuck to the sides was soot. He would scrap the soot off of the sides of the cylinder and add it to water. Before the soot and water would mix he would have to add just a touch of shampoo. The shampoo acted as a bonding agent. Without shampoo the two would never mix. That's how the ink was made and it only came in black. The thinner it was mixed the grayer it was, the thicker the darker.

To sterilize the needles we would burn the end and throw them away after they had been used. We would put the ink in a toothpaste cap that was thoroughly cleaned with antibacterial soap and alcohol pads. Before we started, we would round up antibacterial ointment so we would have what we needed to be sure we could properly take care of the tattoo once it was done. We took every precaution to ensure the cleanest environment possible. I can't say the same for the rest of the inmate population. I have seen some prisoners use the same needle over and over. Some of them would even share their needles and ink even after it had been setting for days. I saw the stagnated blood in the caps of ink on several different occasions. It was unbelievable to think that these people cared so little about themselves. It's no wonder prison tattoos are frowned upon.

The person I had the most in common with, and who became my closest friend, was Paul, but we all called him "Convict". He was around 47 years old and was as funny as he was loyal. When he was 16 years old he had gotten into a fight in an abandon school where he and a few other boys were hanging out. During the fight the other boy ended up falling out of the second story window and dying. Convict ended up doing eight years in prison for it. When he was 24, he was released and began working in the coal mines. When the guys he was working with found out he had just gotten out of prison, they started calling him Convict and the name stuck. For twenty years he had worked in the mines and raised two children. He and I had a lot in common, especially our sense of humor. I saw so much of my father in him. The things he knew, the jokes he told, even the way he spoke and the words he used.

The first time I met Convict I was maybe ten years old. My father and I were out on one of our weekend drives; we passed Convict and his girlfriend-soon to become his wife-headed in the opposite direction. It was a beautiful summer day and he was driving a red Camaro with the T-tops out. Dad turned around and ran him down after several miles of chasing him. I can hear dad laughing and what he said as he was trying to flag him down. "He's got that woman with him and he doesn't want to stop." Eventually he got him to pull over. We pulled in behind him and as dad got out of the car he looked at me and told me to, "Watch this." As my father approached the car, Convict got out to meet him. By this time I was out as well. They said their hello's and Dad asked "who do you have with you" as he walked up to the driver's side door. He looked at the woman through the missing T-tops and said, "Damn, Convict this woman ain't ugly." Even at ten years old I thought it was funny as hell.

After one of my presentencing hearings, my mother and aunt were on their way home when they were involved in a car accident. It was over an hour drive back to my mother's house. It was common for her to recline her seat to take a nap. My aunt was driving and had either blacked out or fallen asleep which caused her to drift into the other lane and hit a truck head on. Neither my aunt nor the driver of the truck was seriously injured, but my mother had ruptured her spleen and broken her back. Because of the way she was reclined in the seat, the lap belt held her and the shoulder harness stopped her instantly- which caused everything in-between to keep moving. She was shot forward with such force that she was more or less folded into the wrong way. She had to have her spleen removed and went through more surgeries than I was able to keep track of. She was hospitalized for six months.

I didn't even know she was involved in an accident until the next day. I was taken to one of the non-contact visiting rooms where most of my family was waiting. I remember thinking on the way up the hall that it had to be my attorney coming to tell me they were going let me go. I had never been taken out of the pod at that time of night and could tell the CO's were acting nicer than usual. I thought it was because I was going home. So when I saw all my family there, and not my mother, I went from high expectations, to a sickening feeling of dread.

When I walked into the little room they told me the news and assured me she was ok. They said the reason they had not been up the day it happened was because they didn't know the extent of her injuries. When they came they wanted to be able to tell me more than she was in a car accident. They told me all they knew and we made a plan so I could call my aunt's cell phone. I could only make collect calls from jail but my aunt was more or less at the hospital all the time. If I could get her on her cell phone then I could speak to my mother.

It took a week before I was able to reach my aunt while she as at the hospital. She took mom her phone and I spoke with her for maybe two minutes before the CO in the tower cut the phone off. I was beyond pissed! I hit the call button in the pod so I could speak to the tower officer. I told him the phone was not working and that's when he told me he was the one who cut the phone off. My fifteen minutes were up, and he would not cut it back on nor would he call the shift supervisor to come and speak to me. My only other option was to make them come. I took the decision out of his hands when I started trying to kick the window out of the front door. It took me about ten minutes of steady kicking, but eventually the shift supervisor came. When I told him what had happened, he reprimanded the tower officer and had him turn the phone back on. After I spoke with my mother, I went back to the intercom in the pod and hit the button. I told the CO that cut the phone off that the first chance I had I was going to beat his teeth out and there was nothing he could do about it.

He took my threat as serious as it was, and reported it to the administration. There were some Correctional Officers that took advantage of their position and the authority that was entrusted to them. They were insecure with their masculinity. These guys were especially bold when they had the security of a door protecting them. What they failed to realize was that sooner or later they would have to face these same guys they were bullying. I loved seeing them trying to eat their words and choking on them, but the first chance they got they were right back at it but it was usually someone else.

Convict and Dotson had been transferred to prison months before. When I was told to pack my things I thought I was going there as well. I wasn't told where I was going until I was on my way. A week after the phone call incident, I was transferred to another regional jail. I was only there for about a month before I was finally taken to prison. I had spent twenty-five months in regional jails, and as sad as it sounds, couldn't wait to get to prison. It was probably a good thing they transferred me when they did because I had already made up my mind to whip that CO's ass the first time I saw him. In reality it probably saved me another charge.

For two years I was told how much better prison was compared to the regional jails. I heard stories about working out, playing baseball and basketball, and doing pretty much whatever I wanted, as long as I wasn't acting too crazy. I was excited to finally be on my way. If only half of the stories were true, I would be much better off. Plus I was going to get to see Convict and Dotson again.

Chapter 24

The prison I was moved to was called Mountain Top Correctional Complex. It got the name because it was built on top of an old strip job that was located on the tallest mountain within a hundred miles. As we drove up the first thing I saw was the tower. Between the moon and night sky it looked menacing. It also looked a lot taller than it really was, because of the absence of any kind of back ground to compare it to. I remember silently saying to myself, *well, here you are, you wanted to be a tough guy*. This is where they keep them. I don't know why I remember that. Maybe it's because of the ridiculous way I perceived things to be, compared to the way they actually were. They were so shockingly different that it stuck with me as a reminder to not jump to conclusions, and put aside preconceived notions.

Three of us were taken to prison that day. When we got there we were lined up, stripped, sprayed with some kind of disinfecting chemical, and told to shower. Like the regional jail we were photographed from head to toe, with emphasis on our tattoos and scars. Along with photo documentation, the significance of our tattoos and how we got certain scars were recorded in a written log. We were also fingerprinted and new mug-shots taken. Before we were moved to our new cells, we were taken to medical where they took blood for DNA filing and checked for diseases. We had to stay in a receiving pod for a month before we could be released into general population. We were told it was because they weren't sure we would be staying at MTCC and to be reasonably certain they wouldn't be putting us in any known danger. I was celled with one of the two guys that came in with me.

    Once we were in the cell together I started asking about his charges. He told me he was in for robbery, but in reality the only thing he took was a child's innocence. I explained my concerns to him, and told him that I wanted to see his paper work or some proof of his charges. At first he said he didn't have anything with his charges on it. I reminded him of the paper we had to sign before we took the DNA test. It had our names, D.O.C. numbers and charges on them. They also gave us a copy of it. When he said he threw that away I knew he was a child molester. Before I could say another word, there was four CO's at my cell telling my new cell mate that he had to come with them. When they brought him back they told me if I beat him up or even harassed him they would bury me in lock-up. I hadn't been there a hot minute and I was already being threatened with lock-up. I should have known it was a sign of things to come. I was a little intimidated at first. But after a few minutes of going over all the possible consequences, I decided I wasn't going to live with a child molester. I had the bright idea, that if I could get him to ask to be moved I wouldn't get in any trouble. Plus I could make his life miserable for a while, and in some way pay my respects to that little kid he scared for the rest of his life. For thirty- three days I gave him hell. He took it like someone weak and sick enough to touch kids would. Sometimes I couldn't help but see him do it in my mind. I wanted to slap the shit out of him so bad; I think I made myself more miserable than I made him. Instead of beating him, I drew a circle in the corner of our cell and made him stick his nose in it. I would make him stay like that until I could get the image out of my head.

When we first arrived it was in the middle of an institutional shake down. That's when the entire prison is locked down. Every cell is searched one by one for anything and everything that we were not supposed to have. For seventeen days I was kept in my cell, no shower, no rec, and no phone calls. On top of that I was stuck in that little 8x10 cell with a child molester. When it came time for us to be searched, we were strip searched and our few belongings gone through with a fine tooth comb. When you are new you don't have much to be searched. The only thing they could find to bitch about was a map of the world. The child molester had brought it with him from the regional jail and it only named the different countries, nothing with any kind of detail. They acted as though it was a blueprint for escape. Nothing was done about it and we were released to the yard. Come to find out eighty percent of the inmates on the yard were sex offenders.

I had a new state appointed attorney for my appeal. I had been waiting on him to finish it for two years, but he was in no hurry. Since my conviction all I heard was appeal this and appeal that. I tried to read and learn what I could about the law, but the law library at the regional jail was sorely lacking. What they did have was a copy of the constitution. I knew if I could find a constitutional violation I would for sure get a new trial. I found out that the police using the confidential informant was a violation of my Fifth Amendment rights. After months and months of fighting, arguing, writing, and calling, my attorney finally sent me a copy of a rough draft he drew up of my appeal. What amazed me was there was no mention of the Circuit Clerk's involvement or the use of the confidential informant. I had to threaten to fire him before he would add anything about the Fifth Amendment violation.

He had also portrayed me as a bad guy that was convicted, not because of any evidence, but because of my past. He wrote in the rough draft that "even men of bad character are entitled to a fair trial." I had told him to add the constitutional violation and to take the "bad character" line out, because it would surely be used against me at some point. I did like the angle of even bad guys deserving a fair trial and shouldn't be convicted based on their past, or unrelated acts or actions. There was just something about that "bad character" line that really bothered me. He told me he would take it out and add the violation of my Fifth Amendment rights, because the confidential informant was never produced. He did add the Fifth Amendment violation, but he did not take the bad character line out. I was pissed, but if it helped get me a new trial-then so what.

It was eight months before I got the news that the Supreme Court agreed to hear my case. That was half the battle. During this time my mother received some money from the car accident she was in. She immediately hired an attorney to write the brief for my appeal and to argue it in front of the Supreme Court. After my new attorney read the appeal, he pointed out a lot of things that my state appointed appeal lawyer should have noted but hadn't. The brief could only be about what was in the appeal and nothing else. He said he would try to work in certain issues, but thought the Supreme Court wouldn't go for it. After the brief was submitted, a date for oral arguments was scheduled.

During the oral arguments my attorney did the best he could. Every time he tried to slip in anything that wasn't in the original appeal, one of the Judges would remind him he wasn't allowed do that and to keep to the topics in the appeal. The Supreme Court judges did, however, ask a lot of questions. After the hearing a few of the Judges came down and introduced themselves to my family. My family and attorney were sure they would grant me a new trial. Since I wasn't there, I had to rely on the information they gave me. I was very hopeful that I would be getting out of prison and my innocence would be proven.

While I was waiting to hear the Supreme Court decision I ended up going to lock up for "compromising" a nurse. She said I had been sexually inappropriate. The sad thing was it was all a lie. I did, however, get a few cigarettes from her, but she was so damn ugly I wouldn't have screwed her if I could have. She had been inappropriate with at least one of the prisoners that was working in medical, and she thought if she told on someone it would take the heat off her. Or at least that was the only reason I could come up with as to why she would do what she did. Besides what could I really say? She had been giving me cigarettes and I was guilty of compromising her. This way she was in no danger of getting in trouble. If she told that she was bringing me cigarettes she would be fired. If she was the innocent victim of an unwanted sexual advance, then she was just doing her job by writing me up.

I wrote to my Legal Rep on the yard and asked him to go and talk to the guy she was involved with and to take two of my friends with him. I ended up beating the ridiculous compromising charge. The investigators, however, did intercept the letter I wrote to my Legal Rep. They wrote me up for assault because they said the note was really about me putting a hit out on the guy. They said talking didn't really mean talking since I told my Legal Rep to take two other guys with him.

On top of that the investigators also wrote up my Legal Rep and two friends. Even though they knew they had never seen the letter nor did anything wrong. I went back to kangaroo court and argued my case the best I could. With the investigators changing the definition of words and me not having their dictionary I didn't stand a chance. The investigator always thought there was some kind of hidden message in everything. What the dumbasses failed to realize was there wasn't. What people needed to say they usually said straight up and said it right in front of them, because we all knew that was the best way to hide it. They would usually miss the point by trying to find something that wasn't there. I had made my mind up that as long as my Legal Rep and two friends got their write ups dropped, I would take the blame. They were dead after me anyway, and all they could give me was sixty days. Besides in my mind I was getting out as soon as my appeal came through, so they could kiss my ass.

I did the sixty days and then the administration put me in segregation, because they said I was a security risk. They only wanted child molesters, rapists, and people they could bully on the yard. Since I was none of those, I was placed on what they called "the program." It was basically lock-up, but after four months you could have a T.V. That is, if you could afford one. If you didn't have the money or wouldn't "work for them" you were shit out of luck. What I mean by "work for them" is to give the administration information and agree to rat on anyone you could gather information on. It's no wonder everyone started getting stabbed, but the administration would never take the blame for that.

I called home every chance I got, hoping to hear the Supreme Court made their decision and my conviction was over turned. I was on "the program" for six months when I got the news. I was at rec when I got to call home. I could tell immediately mom had heard something. Her voice and attitude were completely different. When she told me my appeal had been turned down, I was devastated. It was like I had been kicked in the stomach. My knees buckled and an overpowering feeling of helplessness and confusion came over me. It was like all of the oxygen had been sucked out of my lungs. There were a thousand questions running through my mind and no answers to be had. There was no one I could talk to or call that could tell me anything I wanted to hear or needed to know. I couldn't believe it. It was even worse than when I was convicted. I felt like my life was over. I had everything riding on that appeal.

Chapter 25

It was a good two weeks before I could think clear enough to consider what my next move was going to be. It was probably a good thing I was in segregation. It gave me time to process what was going on without the aggravation of having to explain it to anyone. The last thing I wanted was to have to face people. I had been telling everyone I was innocent and my appeal was going to set me free. I was not only crushed, I was embarrassed as well. Embarrassed because I was made into a liar by the very people who I thought was going to prove my innocence. The one good thing that came from my appeal was that one of the Supreme Court Justices wrote a descent in my favor saying, "Mr. Pangloss did not receive a fair trial. It wasn't even close."

The next step in the legal process was to file a habeas corpus petition. To do this my mother spent even more money to hire another attorney. This new attorney was going to be my trial lawyer if the direct appeal had been granted. That is if I would have been granted a new trial. With the new fire report (that I'll explain more about in a minute) and all of the Prosecutor's crooked tricks exposed, I didn't think there would be another trial. By this time my mother had spent fifty thousand dollars and I was no closer to getting out, than the day I went in. My new attorney went right to work and within a few months had filed the paperwork for my habeas corpus.

The two judges in McDowell County didn't want to be involved with my Habeas Corpus, and stepped down as the judges in my case. The Supreme Court then had to appoint another judge to oversee my hearing. Since every step in the court system takes time, and having judges step down was not a common occurrence, it took even longer than usual. All I could do was wait.

I had been in segregation for damn near three years when one day out of the blue I get a letter from Mom. It had a cover page and in big black boxed print it says, "SIT DOWN. OUR PRAYERS HAVE BEEN ANSWERED." Before I read a word of her letter my mind was running wild with hope and confusion. In her letter she told me she had gotten a call from the McDowell County Commissioner. He was one of the few politician's that hadn't turned against my mother. He said the Prosecutor contacted him and wanted to know if he knew why my attorney hadn't filed the paperwork to schedule a hearing requesting the charges against me be dropped and for my immediate release from prison. He said an investigation had been conducted by the foremost fire expert in the country and his investigation proved my innocence. He said, "The fire was not incendiary, but electrical. The State Fire Marshal had been wrong on all accounts."

I don't remember what the rest of the letter said. I do remember the feeling it gave me. I was overcome by a flood of emotions. It was relief, joy, vindication, happiness, and gratefulness, all rolled into one. I began to not cry, but to weep. Finally after all I had been through, the suffering and loss, my innocence could be proven.

It took me a week before I could get a hold of my attorney. When I finally did get in touch with him, he wasn't nearly as excited as I expected. My mother had sent him a copy of the new fire investigator's report, but instead of him trying to make a motion for my immediate release he said he would amend the habeas petition and send it to the judge. I could not believe what I was hearing. I was crushed. I just knew they were going to come and open my cell door. I was expecting to be told how sorry they were, and I was free to go.

I spoke with prisoners who I knew were familiar with the law. They all had different opinions on how to proceed. The one constant thing I did hear was how the state was going to have to pay me for every day I spent imprisoned. It didn't take long before the entire prison population heard about the new investigations. It became the main topic of every conversation I had. It didn't take long before it lost its allure. I was sick of talking about it, but everyone seemed to be genuinely happy for me. The one thing that got on my nerves was when they started throwing around these astronomical numbers the state would have to pay me for wrongful imprisonment. I did believe I would be compensated in some way for all of the time that was taken from me. I had been in prison for almost eight years and no amount of money could buy back the time I had lost.

It took another five months before I went to court for my habeas hearing. I hadn't left the prison since I had gotten there five years earlier. The first thing I noticed was how much more colorful everything was. The colors were brighter and more vibrant than I remembered. I also took notice to how much smaller the cars had gotten. Not only that but how poor my eye sight had gotten as well. I couldn't read the road signs until I was right up on them. The possibilities of my future were endless; if only I was a free man. My eye sight wasn't so poor that I couldn't see that.

The hearing went well considering the Prosecuting Attorney lied when the truth would have sufficed. When asked about the new investigation, and how it was completely different from what was testified to at trial, his answer was totally different from what was in the report. What was even more disturbing was my attorney didn't catch, or call him on it. I couldn't fathom how the most important piece of evidence I had was being disregarded like it was. It was a ten page report. If my new lawyer who was supposed to have been so damn good, couldn't successfully read and argue a ten page document, then I didn't need him. He should have called the Prosecutor on his blatant lies, and ask him why he was being so deceptive. The end of the hearing the judge said he would consider all the evidence and asked for a few pieces of information to be sent to him. I was told the Judge didn't have a time limit on making his decision; so back to prison I went.

A few days later I got a letter from my cousin, Jessie, saying he had run into my old girlfriend, Billie Jo. Except for my dad, Jessie is the only person that knew about my relationship with her. I had told him years later during one of my drunken binges. I could have told Jessie back when she and I were hooking up, and I would have never had to worry about him telling anyone. She had given him her address to give to me and said that she would love to hear from me- if I wanted to write. As soon as I read his letter I wrote to her. She was so wonderfully sweet; I was completely taken back by how great she truly was. It wasn't long before my days revolved around getting her letters. I would set for hours waiting on the CO's to come around with the mail. If I didn't get mail from her my mood, along with the whole day, was ruined. Since it was so expensive to call North Carolina, Billie Jo got a separate phone with a West Virginia number just for us. When the phone calls went from ten dollars for a fifteen minute call to seventy-five cents, we began talking more and more.

It wasn't long before I realized how special she was. She was something so rare and unheard of I began calling her my "Unicorn." Every time I called I would catch myself holding my breath until she answered. When she answered and I heard her voice I would start smiling like a school boy. No matter how bad of a mood I was in, just to hear her say hello was enough to turn my world around. I went from fighting with the CO's every day to trying to avoid them if I couldn't get along with them. She started coming to see me even though it took her four hours to get there. If I were to get in trouble or written up, my phone calls and visitation privileges would have been taken away. I forgot about the walls and all my problems once I got to see her. We had been together for a year and I still hadn't been able to hug or kiss her. When she came to see me we would have to talk on a phone while I sat behind a glass wall. I had requested to just be allowed to hug her after our visit was over, and was denied every time. I watched other inmates that were in the same situation I was in get contact visits week after week.

They got to hug; kiss, take pictures, and set with their family and friends during their visits and none of them drove as far as Billie did. Half of them were child molesters, and the other half rats. I was neither, so I got no such treatment.

The main topic of most of our conversations was what we were going to do when I got out, where we were going to go, and how we were going to get there. We talked about high school and what we had been doing since. She had a little girl and she told me about her, and how much she loved being a mother. I grew to love her more and more each day.

Chapter 26

It was noon on a Tuesday, thirteen months after my hearing when I received the news. I called Billie Jo and she asked if I had spoken to my mother. I told her I had not, and she told me to call my mom then call her back. Mom answered the phone yelling "You're coming home, you're coming home." When she calmed down she told me all the details and developments. I found out the judge ordered my conviction to be overturned. She had received a call from my attorney, who told her the prosecutor had dropped all charges saying he would not retry my case.

Wednesday morning I walked out of prison a free man. Billie Jo was waiting on me as I walked out the gate. She ran to me and gave me the first kiss we had gotten to share since she came back into my life. As soon as I stepped through the last gate and out into the world, all my troubles felt like they had been washed away. For the first time Billie and I had nothing keeping us apart, whether it was bars, walls, or a boyfriend. We were free to do what we wanted, how we wanted. No one could tell me what I could do or where I could go. I had a new start and outlook on life. I was tired of being told what to do. Now, I could decide on my own.

I was scared to touch Billie at first. I thought I may hurt her or break her or something. I had been in prison for eight years and in solitary confinement for four of it. I had forgotten how to interact with people. As strange as it may sound, I felt uncomfortable not having hand-cuffs and shackles on. It felt weird not being behind a metal door and stuck in a tiny cell. I did, however, feel more comfortable around her than I did anyone else; but something is not right when you're scared to touch your girlfriend.

A few weeks after I was out I started looking for an attorney to take my case for wrongful imprisonment. I called and went to dozens of lawyers. No one wanted to even attempt to sue the county or state. I can't say I wasn't disappointed, because I was. I was counting on that money for my new start in life. Living costs money, and to everyone who knew me I would always be a murderer. For me there would be no vindication. That money was my consolation and pacifier while I was being held captive. I had dreams and made plans of where I was going to go, along with all the things I was going to do. When Billie came back into my life and I got to hold and touch her, money didn't seem all that important anymore.

I had managed to put back enough money to buy a motorcycle and take a vacation. We rode down to the Florida Keys and spent a week together, doing absolutely nothing. The smell of the ocean and the wind on my face is a memory I will never forget. The water was crystal clear and the sand so hot it burnt my feet. Billie was even more beautiful with her hair a mess and no make-up. It was perfect.

In the end I never got a penny from the county or state. Hell, I never got so much as an "I'm sorry". What I ended up with was a story, this book, and *One Look*.

ONE LOOK

What would it be like to be someone else?

To see the world through their eyes and look back at myself.

Would I be happy at what I would see,

Or would I even realize it was me?

There's times I would be happy, and even proud,

Seeing the man I was bound.

Other times I would be disgusted, disappointed, and even ashamed,

Not recognizing the man I became.

My heart is heavy, I try to hide my face.

Hating my life, the world, and my place.

How could I have fallen so far so fast?

Not seeing the present, but living in the past.

Never knowing the cause of my misdeeds,

Especially the pain that they bring.

That is not the man I was meant to become.

Having lost touch with my feelings being so numb.

I know I will overcome my failed attempts,

There is no satisfaction in being content.

I will be my own hero and write my own book.

Be my own man, and take advantage of that look!

www.ingramcontent.com/pod-product-compliance
Lightning Source LLC
Chambersburg PA
CBHW051758040426
42446CB00007B/426